20th Anniversary Edition

When His
Secret Sin
Breaks Your
Heart

D0370142

Kathy Gallagher

When His
Secret Sin
Breaks Your
Heart

www.purelifeministries.org

For more books and other teaching
resources please contact:

Pure Life Ministries
14 School Street
Dry Ridge, KY 41035
(888) PURELIFE
www.purelifeministries.org

SPECIAL
ACKNOWLEDGEMENT

I have some dear friends in life, but, besides my husband, I would have to say that Carol Bourque is my best friend. I call her my "best" friend because of all that we have been through together.

I have watched her cry, struggle and agonize her way through the devastation of her marriage. She bravely worked her way through, inch by inch, the painful process of letting go of the "happily ever after" scenario she hoped and prayed for. She has faced her own failures and mistakes and fought to keep Jesus Christ at the center of everything.

Carol Bourque is the Director of Women's Counseling for Pure Life Ministries because she has proven herself to be a faithful follower of Christ no matter what the cost. For the past ten years she has poured herself into the lives of other women. She truly exemplifies the life of love and unselfishness that I have written about in this book.

I count it a great privilege to work together with her in this vineyard to which the Lord has called us.

DEDICATION

This book is dedicated to my beloved.
How far we have come, from ashes to beauty.
The Lord has made our crooked paths straight,
and you have become to me the love of God personified.
Thank you for loving me and being faithful to me.
Truly my beloved is mine, and I am his.

TABLE OF CONTENTS

INTRODUCTION

It has been twenty years since I wrote the original version of *When His Secret Sin Breaks Your Heart*. A lot of hurting women have crossed my path in the intervening decades. Yet nothing I have encountered since then has led me to deviate from the ancient truths the Lord revealed to me regarding being married to someone dealing with sexual sin. As difficult as this subject is, God is still, and will always be, not just the One with the answers but is Himself the answer that we long for.

When I first penned this book, I chose to utilize a unique format for addressing the host of different issues hurting wives face—responding to questions women have asked me in the form of individual letters. In this 20th Anniversary edition, I chose to address many topics in a more traditional method, adding nine chapters of new material. As a result, I have discarded a few of the original letters, but most have been retained in the second part of this new edition.

Even as I have added new material in an attempt to handle the variety of issues hurting wives experience, please understand that I haven't touched on every issue wives may face—that would be impossible, as no two women have had the exact same experience. In fact, this is definitely not a one-size-fits-all kind of book, so you may find yourself looking for those pieces that apply to your situation.

While this book does not provide formulas for "fixing" your husband, it does address practical situations you probably deal with on a regular basis. But the main thing I wanted to emphasize throughout the book is how IMPORTANT it is that you see Jesus in your situation. Having practical answers is secondary to this.

One of the subjects woven throughout the pages of this book is true biblical love—how to respond to pain with love rather than hate; how to replace bitterness with compassion; how to intercede rather than fret, and so on. Of course the earnest believer wants to be purged of ungodly attitudes and desires nothing more than to act in a way that both honors and pleases the Lord.

Another prevalent theme you will find in these pages is the importance of suffering in the believer's life. As you come to see the precious work it is producing in you, you will begin to appreciate it—even embrace it! This is the sublime truth Paul the Apostle alluded to when he wrote, "For momentary, light affliction is producing for us an eternal weight of glory." (2 Corinthians 4:17) Paul experienced far more suffering than any of us and he knew what he was talking about!

Over the years I have run across books that express in great detail the sufferings of the woman married to a sexual addict. My concern over those books has been that they haven't offered the anguished wife anything other than shallow empathy. The overriding message spun by these authors is: "You are a victim and your husband is a perpetrator! God wants to bless you! Get rid of this loser so you can get on with your life!" It is the very kind of "me first" attitude one would expect from our fallen culture. As a woman who has been through it and lived around it for most of my adult life I can tell you that there is something far richer and more meaningful than saving your own life.

My experience has been that those who prefer the easier solutions and pat answers offered by popular psychology rather than biblical solutions usually suffer most in the end. Dealing with life's problems God's way may often seem difficult, but those who choose to do so always reap the benefits in the end. A new person emerges, not because of any self-esteem revival, but as a result of having found the presence of the Lord to be sufficient through every trial and every struggle.

Ultimately, we are all on a journey and while this trial might seem like a huge detour to you, I want to assure you that it is the Lord's desire to use all of this to bring forth an inner joy that transcends outward circumstances. I want to encourage you to let the Master Architect of the freeway system you find yourself on guide you safely through to the end.

MY STORY

In January of 1979, after several years of physical abuse, while married to a prospect of the Hells Angels, being involved with another man was the farthest thing from my mind. I finally felt free—free from the tyranny of a controlling husband, free from the fear in which I had constantly lived, and free from the abuse. I had a job, my own car, and most importantly, my own life.

But a few months prior to this, I had to flee for my life when I left my husband. He was a ruthless man and I was terrified of him. I remained incognito until things had calmed down with him enough so that I could resume my friendship with his older brother, Gale, and his wife, Joanne.

It was at their home in Sacramento one day that I first met Steve Gallagher. I was warming myself by the heater when he came waltzing through the front door of their little shack. My first impression of him was that he seemed out of place in that environment. Steve was a real estate agent and had come to the house because Gale had shown interest in buying a home. Steve and Gale had done drugs and crime together in their earlier years but had not kept in touch with each other.

It never crossed my mind that I would someday become involved with this man. He was twenty-four, and I was only eighteen. He seemed so old to me. At any rate, as I began running into him at their house over the next few weeks, he began to show an interest in me. Steve later told me that, from the first time we met, he knew we were meant for each other. I didn't share this feeling and really had no desire to go out with him. Nevertheless, at Gale and Joanne's insistence, I finally agreed to a date.

He picked me up in his spacious Ford LTD and whisked me off to a drive-in movie. Before we had even gotten to the movie, he expressed his desire that I sit next to him. I informed him right off the bat that I felt no obligation to cuddle up beside a perfect stranger. So, our first date ended in an argument, with me angrily storming out of his car when he finally took me home. He yelled for me to come back, which I did, and after he humbled himself, and politely suggested we start all over again, I reluctantly agreed.

We continued to go out together over the next few weeks. One day, he asked me to go with him to a beachside resort in Santa Cruz for a weekend—just the two of us. I knew what that meant: we would be in the same hotel room together for an entire weekend. This was heavy-duty. To me, it meant commitment; it meant that I was giving myself to him—I had to drop my guard and give my heart to him. I was very uneasy and unsure that I was ready to take the plunge. I think I even asked him, "Will we stay in the same room together?" I just wanted to make sure we understood each other. This was a huge decision for me, one of the biggest of my adult life. In my mind, consenting to go was the same as saying "yes" to a marriage proposal. If I gave myself to him, it meant that I was his and he was mine. This wasn't just a date or a fun weekend with some guy that I liked. I had never done anything like this with anyone. Yet, in some way, I felt as though I was being pulled helplessly and irresistibly into this relationship. I finally agreed.

We were both full of excitement and had an absolutely wonderful time. You guessed it: I had fallen in love with "Prince Charming." Actually, I think I had loved Steve long before that weekend, but it was in Santa Cruz that I knew for sure I wanted to spend the rest of my life with him.

When we returned home on Sunday, we immediately moved in together. I was on cloud nine at first, but soon I began to see what Steve was really like. Full of ambition, he worked night and day in real estate. He was bent on becoming successful which drove him to put undue pressure upon himself. This resulted in a short temper at home. I attributed his impatience with me to the stress of his real estate business and hoped that he would eventually change.

Despite all of this, a very interesting thing began to happen between us: Steve started to talk to me about God. He shared with me that he had first come to the Lord when he was doing jail time as a sixteen-year-old but had backslidden shortly thereafter. He said that one day he wanted to get right with God again.

This was all news to me, but I immediately came under conviction because we had been living in sin together. Over the next few months, I lived with a sense of condemnation—that I was in trouble with God. Yet, I didn't really know what to do about it.

Then, one day, I met Brother Jess at my sister's house. He was a sweet, Southern Baptist pastor who told me that I was a sinner in need of a Savior. The Lord had thoroughly prepared me for this divine appointment, and I made Jesus the Lord and Master of my life that day. The next day, I packed up all my belongings and left Steve.

Well, I fell in love with the Lord. I was on fire for Jesus. He became the center of my life. I spent hours reading the Word, awestruck by its profound wisdom and revelation of future events. I was in church whenever the doors opened and almost single-handedly turned that little church upside-down, infecting everyone with my newfound joy. Everywhere I went I talked to others about God. People couldn't believe the change that had come over me—I was a different person.

One day, zealous to see people come to know the Lord, I called Steve to try to witness to him. I wanted him to have what I had, but the years of being backslidden had hardened him to the things of God. When I had left him "for the Lord," he felt betrayed by God. At the end of our conversation, completely out of the blue, he told me to pray about whether we should be married. This was unthinkable! He was dead to spiritual realities, while I was completely happy serving God as a single Christian. Nevertheless, his words kept ringing in my ears over the next couple of weeks. I couldn't seem to escape them.

A month later, in January 1980, we were married. I had been a Christian for about five months. At first, he began attending church with me. Little by little though, he drifted away from God, once again, unwilling to fully surrender to the Lord.

Even though Steve was far more refined than my first husband, he was more difficult to live with. He never physically abused me, but I feared him more than my ex-husband who, as I mentioned before, was very abusive. Steve had a seething, violent anger that was always contained just under the surface. I saw him as the sort of person who could snap and just start killing people at random.

His anger—always directed at me—came through his sharp, cutting tongue. He was extremely critical and sarcastic. He would ridicule me whenever I did things wrong. I could never seem to satisfy him or do anything right. This, of course, left deep, emotional wounds that hurt far more than my first husband's fists.

Nevertheless, I tried to hope for the best. I knew that much of his frustration was due in part to the fact that the real estate market had suffered a tremendous blow with escalating interest rates. As a result, Steve's career, which he had worked so hard to establish, began to crumble. No longer able to continue in real estate, he began looking for job opportunities elsewhere.

This took us to Los Angeles where Steve began the long, excruciating process of becoming a deputy sheriff. Instead of our lives improving, the stress of being on the Department made things even worse. He became even more abusive to me. Unfortunately, I sought Steve's approval, rather than God's. I became weaker and more dependent on him. Gradually, I too backslid. I would make feeble attempts to read my Bible and pray, but I had no strength or hunger inside. I had long since quit going to church.

Not long after we moved to Los Angeles, I found out that he had been addicted to pornography for years. He also let me know that he had been visiting massage parlors and prostitutes. He explained that the reason he was telling me about his secret life was because he wanted it to end. He reasoned that if we watched porn movies together, it would not only enhance our sex life, but it would also keep him from going out on me. Needless to say, I was crushed. I now realized I had to compete with women in pornographic movies and magazines. The whole thing was devastating to me, but instead of turning to God, I tried even harder to please Steve.

I intensely pursued his affection and love more than ever. I would have days when I felt like my heart would literally burst from the pain and rejection I felt. Other days, usually when he was sweet to me, I held out hope that he would change.

Unfortunately, allowing porn into our marriage bed did not improve our marriage; it only drove him to demand more. To keep up with his insatiable appetite for sex, we eventually began getting sexually involved with other people. The only way I could handle the complete loss of my own dignity and self-respect was to drown them in drugs. I became addicted to methamphetamine.

After several years of doing everything I could to win Steve, I finally gave up. I had loved him so much and had been willing to do literally anything to keep him, but his obsession with illicit sex had become insane. Having lost all hope, I left him and filed for divorce. I was devastated. Not only had I lost the battle to win him, but I had completely given up all my morals and self-respect in the meantime. I had to face what I had become.

It was then, almost like a miracle from God, that I met a guy named Tim. After years of emotional abuse, he was like a breath of fresh air! Immediately I forgot all the pain. Being with him helped me to stick my head in the sand and forget the loss I had suffered.

Tim was so good to me. He opened car doors for me, treated me with kindness and respect, and made me laugh a lot. Unlike Steve, he was very sensitive and considerate. Another thing I really appreciated was the way he would open up to me. This never happened with either of my husbands.

My involvement with Tim lasted for several weeks. Almost immediately I began sleeping with him, deceiving myself into believing that God would understand, because we really loved each other. His continuous drinking and quick willingness to be in adultery should have caused me to doubt his sincerity as a Christian, but I was so enthralled with him that I stifled my nagging doubts.

I had no contact with Steve during this time, so I didn't know that when I left he had gone back to his old ways of chasing girls. One morning, unbeknownst to me, he woke up in the apartment of one of his girlfriends, feeling the emptiness of his life. All that day he was miserable. That afternoon he went to work at the jail, but it was a busy evening, so he didn't get back to eat his supper in the deputy chow hall until late. There were no other deputies there when he finally arrived. As he sat there, eating in miserable silence, a deputy named Willy strolled in. He, too, was late arriving and somehow the conversation got around to Steve's struggles. Upon hearing that Willy was a Christian, he poured out his heart to him, telling him how empty and unhappy he felt in life. Willy suggested that Steve give his heart to the Lord, which he did.

"I felt like a thousand pounds lifted off my back!" Steve exclaimed. "But it didn't last long. When I got home that night, all I could think about was getting my wife back. I tossed and turned all night, upset about Kathy. In the middle of the night I heard a voice tell me that she would call in the morning. I didn't know if I was hearing things or what!"

The very next morning I took Tim to work, but after I dropped him off, I did a very strange thing: I started driving north on the freeway toward the San Fernando Valley where Steve and I had lived. I had no idea why I was doing this; it seemed like someone else was steering the car. When I got to Van Nuys, I stopped at a phone booth and called Steve.

He was very excited to hear from me, telling me what had happened the night before. I was glad to hear of his new life, but I had no intention of going back to him. My feelings for him were dead. I now had what I had wanted for so long. I was convinced that God had brought Tim into my life and I had no desire to go back to Steve. As far as I was concerned, he had lost his opportunity and now the Lord was restoring to me "all the years that the locust had eaten." By this time I was becoming accustomed to being treated like a princess. Tim was giving me the love that I had wanted from Steve; I would be a fool to return to him.

Finally, in desperation, Steve challenged me to call my parents for their advice. This I was more than happy to do, knowing how furious they had become with him when I told them all that he had been doing. I agreed and called them. My dad answered the phone, and when I explained the situation, to my surprise, he told me that the Lord had spoken to them about me. "Kathy," he said earnestly, "you need to go back to your husband." I just sat down in the phone booth and cried. I didn't want to go back to him. I finally pulled myself together and went to his apartment.

The next morning I told Steve that I needed to go get my stuff from Tim's house. He reluctantly agreed to let me go after I called Tim's number and nobody answered. I went there that day and Tim's car was gone. When I let myself in the house, though, I discovered him sitting on the bed. All the charm was gone now; he was furious.

For the next two hours he angrily tried to convince me of what a mistake it would be to go back to Steve. He kept badgering me and I became confused. I knew full well what Steve was like and I didn't want to go back. Tim would vacillate between calm, reasonable arguments and tirades of anger. Finally, in a rage, he ripped my blouse off and forced himself on me. I was so weak and mousey at the time that I let him have his way. In some strange way, it was the thing that brought me back over to Tim.

At his insistence, I finally called Steve. "I don't love you anymore, I love Tim, and I'm not coming back," I coldly told him. When he heard that, he grabbed his off-duty revolver and spun the cylinder around in the mouthpiece so I could hear it. "All right, then you can listen to me blow my brains out!" he shouted.

"Steve, don't do it!" I yelled. When I said that, Tim grabbed my arm. I looked up at him to see the most evil look I had ever seen on anybody's face in all my life. "Kathy, if he wants to kill himself, let him do it. It's not your fault!" It was then I realized that this man I had taken for such a prince was full of the devil.

A pastor had arrived at Steve's apartment and got on the phone with me and asked if he could pray for me. I was terrified and just wanted to get out of that house, but I was afraid to say anything. I told the pastor that I would meet him and Steve at his church and got off the phone. At first, Tim was adamant that I couldn't go, but he could see that I just wanted out of there and, finally, he relented. By the time I made it to where Steve was, it had been over six hours; six hours of hell for both of us.

It took this experience to see what Tim was really like, but it didn't make going back to Steve any easier. It was very difficult for a long time. For the first several months I felt like I had made a huge mistake and I was absolutely crushed: broken over my sinfulness and the shame of being an adulteress, but also because my feelings for Steve were dead. I often felt I would rather be alone than to be with him. I could hardly take it when he would touch me.

To make matters worse, Steve was having a revival in his heart. He was on fire for the Lord and had now fallen deeply in love with me. The affection that I had wanted for so long was now mine in abundance. He was constantly wanting to hold my hand and hug me and kiss me—and I was sick. "Why couldn't you have been like this five years ago?" I would silently exclaim. There were many nights that I cried when we went to bed. I would make sure he didn't know because I didn't want to hurt him, but the truth was: I just didn't want him anymore. I constantly had to fight feelings of disgust.

Gradually, over the months, things got better. We both had so much to overcome. He still had some of the same old attitudes. There were times he would still blame-shift and manipulate, and sometimes even lash out in anger. In spite of his new-found passion for Jesus, he was also still struggling with pornography. But there was a brokenness in Steve now that had never been there before. God was winning in his life.

It took some time for my "feelings" to return. But, gradually they did. Actually, I think God destroyed the old foundation and built a new one, because, when the Lord restored the love and respect that I had lost for Steve, it came back in a brand new way. I started to respect and admire him more than I ever had before. There were times that my love for him became overwhelming; not in the idolatrous way it had been before, but in the love of the Lord. Over the years since we got back together, I have watched Steve allow God to humble him, correct him, and even crush him. Now he truly has become the man of my dreams.

But he wasn't the only one who needed to change. I had to learn to truly put God first in my life also. I came to realize that I had been just as consumed with Steve as he had been with sex. In my own self-centeredness, I had turned to one man after another, looking for fulfillment in life. I gradually learned to turn to God as the center of my life. This didn't make me love Steve less; it simply purified my love for him. Rather than a self-centered "love" which was given with the idea of having my own needs met, I learned to give my husband the unselfish love of the Lord. Our marriage grew stronger and stronger.

Almost immediately, Steve and I began spending time with the Lord every morning. This set a pattern that has lasted for many years. Being in touch with God every day gave me a strength I had never known before. At first, as Steve continued struggling with his addiction to pornography, I became obsessed with his deliverance. God quietly began convicting me of this and kept leading me back to Himself. I soon discovered that the more connected I was with God, the more strength I had to help Steve with his problems.

As I continued to grow in the Lord, I was able to recognize the good that came of failure, instead of seeing it as a catastrophe. Because Steve was serious about his life with God, each fall back into sin served as a blessing in disguise. It deepened the hatred of his sin. Instead of falling apart when he would fail, I became an encouragement to him through those failures. The desire to be supportive of his efforts in this struggle and to keep him accountable in a loving way grew stronger. There was a time when I did not have the maturity or emotional strength to bear him in this way, but the closer I got to the Lord, the more I was able to handle. I came to realize that as long as Steve (or his victory) held the center-stage of my heart, my joy as a person would fall to pieces every time he would fail. But, as I increasingly allowed God the throne of my heart, I found that I now had the strength to help my husband through his failures.

An empty and unsatisfying fling in a massage parlor Steve had in May 1985 proved to be his last one. It took us some time to realize it, but he was free! Now things really began to change. He started becoming the strong one, spiritually. I could actually start leaning on him and confessing my faults to him. We reversed roles: he became my spiritual head and I became a wife who could submit to her "leader" with joy.

What a relief it was when I finally realized I no longer had to look over my shoulder. I still had to continue to repent of my own suspicious nature, but in my heart I knew we had crossed the deep waters of sexual addiction. Now we have a depth in our relationship that very few enjoy. Trusting God in going back to Steve was a turning point in my life, but it was also only the beginning of my own restoration. The restoration of our marriage came about because we both wanted God more than we wanted our own desires.

As I am rewriting this book (in 2018), it has now been 33 years since that last fall on Steve's part, 36 since I reluctantly went back to him, and 38 years since I married him. It was only a year after Steve's last fall in sin that God laid the burden on his heart to begin Pure Life Ministries. Since that time our love for the Lord has intensified and our love for each other has deepened. What God has given me has been worth all of the grief I have endured through the years; not because of my happy marriage but because of what I have in the Lord.

Writing this down in a book doesn't mean the story is over. I only see things getting better and better for both Steve and me, as we both continue to surrender ourselves to God, looking to Him to bring us the fulfillment we desire.

It certainly is true, that there is no pit so deep that the love of God isn't yet deeper.

Part One

WHEN HIS SECRET SIN BREAKS YOUR HEART

1

THE HURTING WIFE

"O Lord, teach me how to handle this
terrible pain in a godly way."

"When he admitted the affair, the first thing I said
to him was, 'But you were my best friend, and you
promised you would never hurt me.'"

— *Cynthia*

"My worst fears were coming true. My husband was
leaving me and I was going to be alone. I instantly
fell apart. I couldn't get out of bed, couldn't eat and
couldn't sleep. I lost about 20 pounds in 3 weeks and
my hair began falling out. I wanted to die."

— *Phyllis*

"One day, my husband confessed to me that he had
been involved homosexually with a young man. I will
never forget that night or the weeks that followed. I
had dealt with a lot of conflicting emotions over the
past 6½ years of our marriage, but this hurt went to
depths I had never experienced before."

— *Karla*

"In a voice filled with anguish and despair, he confessed to me his addiction to pornography. At that moment the pain I felt inside seemed more overwhelming than all that I had previously experienced. It seemed as though I were drowning—being pulled underwater by fear, repulsion, rejection and unrelenting pain. All I knew to do was to cry out to God!"

— Millie

"On October 14th, 2002, my life as I knew it changed forever. Prompted by the Holy Spirit to check the history on his computer, I stared in open-mouthed shock at the filthy and disgusting images of men with men. My first reaction was complete denial: 'This can't be. These are men!'

"Feeling used and manipulated, I vacillated between depression and anger. I suffered from chronic insomnia and some days could hardy muster enough strength to pray. The overwhelming emotions of it all nearly drove me to insanity. I was nothing more than a trophy wife: there to cover the stench of his secret sin!"

— Bonnie

"Early one Saturday morning, he finally confessed to me that he had had an affair with a married woman. I was outraged. I suddenly got up and began to punch him with all of my might.

"The next month was like a nightmare that I couldn't awaken from. More confessions and horror stories: an affair with a 55-year-old woman, masturbation, topless bars, table dances and so on. The blood would run cold through my veins with each story. The left side of my face would go numb. I went from 129 pounds to 113 pounds. My hair began to fall out. I had diarrhea daily, and at times thought that I would surely die. I could not believe that he would be unfaithful to me again. I kept trying to convince myself it was untrue, but there it was, staring me in the face."

— *Kathy*

These stories and hundreds just like them have been my life for the past thirty-two years. They are also a fair representation of what I experienced in my own marriage decades ago. And, I suppose it would be a reasonable assumption that you are reading this book because this is your experience as well.

What could be more shocking than the sudden and unexpected discovery that your husband has a secret obsession with other women—or even men? Perhaps you happened to notice a porn site on the history of your husband's computer or worse, walked in while he was actually viewing one. It's possible you ran across unfamiliar email addresses or phone numbers. Maybe you accidentally found text messages that revealed the awful truth. Or perhaps your husband suddenly made a big confession to you. No matter how you happened upon this crushing discovery, your wound is deep and fresh, the hole in your heart still gaping open like some terrible gash.

You might be one of those women who learned of your husband's unfaithful spirit years ago. The initial shock was eventually replaced with a terrible callousness of despair. Or perhaps the horrific discovery only occurred recently.

When a wife first unearths the appalling truth about her husband's secret life, she feels as though she has been run over by a Mack truck. The pain is overwhelming. Her thoughts swirl around in her mind as if in a blender. It is a mass of painful confusion. One moment she is in a rage toward her husband; the next moment she is engulfed in fear and hopelessness. Sometimes she seems to vividly experience every excruciating sensation while at other times she feels completely numb.

Sorting through these vacillating feelings is very difficult while in the middle of this raging storm.

All of these emotions will be addressed in this book, but for now I want to zero in on four of the most common feelings hurting wives experience.

THE SENSE OF BETRAYAL

One of the first things a wife feels when she discovers her husband's problem is that he has broken the bond of intimacy and trust a husband and wife share.

There really is no easy way to describe the deep sense of betrayal a woman feels. This disloyalty leaves the wife feeling like her husband has abandoned her. The following are some definitions and synonyms of the word abandon: to cast off, discard, drop, scrap, reject, run out on or turn one's back on. Of course, the husband would deny that he is doing this to his wife, but his denials do not change the way she feels.

The truth is that a man cannot cut any deeper into a woman's heart than to take what is so personal and special and give it away to someone else. Sexual intimacy between a husband and wife is the greatest expression of their love for and devotion to each other. Even if the marriage wasn't necessarily great, still, a wife never expects this level of false-heartedness from the one who vowed his love and life to her.

I can remember so well the intense pain I experienced dealing with Steve's unfaithfulness. To me our intimacy was sacred. Saying "I do" at the altar made it exclusive and therefore off-limits to others. He was mine and I was his. What we had together in private was ours, and I was the only one who should know him in that way. Marital sex is the tie that physically binds two individuals together, and its sanctity is due to the spiritual union that is created.

When I found out that Steve was being unfaithful, I was crushed. He was spiritually becoming "one flesh" with anything with a skirt, giving away what was MINE! Our circle of unity had been broken—our marriage bed defiled. We no longer had that special oneness which belonged only to us. Our sexual intimacy had been cheapened—actually nullified—because it was shared with many others. It had little or no value to him because he preferred a cheap thrill to the real thing: me, his wife. The pleasure he wanted from our union could be found or purchased on any street corner or in any massage parlor.

As far as I was concerned there was now nothing left that was ours as a married couple. We were just two people living together, sharing space. It killed me. Day after day the pain of the reality that our marriage was gone swept over me like sea billows. While it was unbearable to me at times, he seemed to be completely impervious to the devastation and misery he was causing.

THE SENSE OF MISTRUST

Tied closely to the feeling of being betrayed is that of being deceived. Like a punch in the gut comes the ugly realization that her husband is two people. She married the man she loved and respected. In her mind she saw the two holding hands (as it were), facing an exciting future together. Now a completely different person has emerged. It is very difficult to reconcile these two distinctly different individuals.

"*Who is this man?*" she asks herself over and over. "How could he look me in the eye and just blatantly lie to me?"

She must now face the horrible reality that he is utterly duplicitous. The man to whom she has committed her life has a completely different life he maintains apart from her. There are other people, places and atmospheres he is involved in that do not correlate with the world they have built together.

She begins to come to grips with the fact that while her husband seems to be living a normal, Christian life, the reality is that he is continually conniving to find a way to sneak back to his beloved sin. The poor wife must now deal with a constant, nagging suspicion about what is really going on inside him.

Another painful fact she must face is that he has been an utter hypocrite. To all of their friends, co-workers, family members and fellow church members he has presented himself as a man who loves his wife and children. His ability to present himself as a respectable, responsible, caring person seemed so effortless. In fact, even she believed him to be a sincere and upright Christian man.

Now she must face the reality that it has all been an act. Perhaps she begins to consider his Christianity in light of the biblical term *hypocrisy.* Jesus could have been speaking of her husband when He said, "You outwardly appear righteous to men, but inwardly you are full of hypocrisy and lawlessness." (Matthew 23:28)

One of the most awful discoveries I have witnessed was what Cindy experienced. She had met Sam in a Bible study and was instantly attracted to him. While he personified manliness, he also ardently promoted his Christianity. She hadn't known him for long when she agreed to marry him, but Christians they knew in common had all vouched for him.

Cindy suspected something wasn't right almost from the beginning. She couldn't put her finger on what was bothering her because it was mostly small unconnected things. For instance, while he acted as though he loved their church, he always seemed to have some critical comment about its leadership. Another thing that surprised her was when he asked her how often she thought they should be intimate. "Why do I have to explain this to him?" she wondered.

One day, while looking for something on his computer, she happened to run across a number of shocking emails he had exchanged with other men. The one that was the most painful to read had been written just prior to their wedding: "I'll be off-line for a few days since I'm getting married." In a more recent email he told some guy that he couldn't meet with him that weekend because he had to spend time with his wife.

She confronted him about her discoveries right away. He told her that he had struggled over the years with homosexuality but promised he would never do it again. "I couldn't understand why he married me when he knew he never intended to be faithful. It was so unjust." Cindy decided to put spyware on his computer while he was at work so she would know the truth about what was going on. "Even though he professed he was not meeting men the spyware told me differently."

THE SENSE OF REJECTION

Another thunderbolt most wives face is the feeling that *they* are the cause of the problem. Perhaps part of the reason this reaction is so common is that our culture puts so much pressure on women to look beautiful. There is something about discovering that one's husband is obsessed with the bodies of other women that strikes at the deepest part of a woman's sense of self-worth.

Cassandra describes what she experienced when she found the websites her husband had been visiting. She raced from one site to the next, trying to understand what was going on with her husband. The whole experience was shocking and humiliating.

We were so in-love! You made me feel like a million bucks. You said there was no one else in this world you wanted but me. You told me all the time how beautiful I was to you. You had all kinds of sweet and endearing nicknames for me. Our beginning was, I thought, a harbinger of things to come.

And then I saw the women who you go to for your sexual thrills. Did it ever occur to you how this would make me feel? How can I compete with the perfect bodies of those porn starlets? There was a time I thought I was pretty and desirable to you, now I can't even bear to look at myself in the mirror. I feel like I'm a mass of blemishes and imperfections. What is wrong with me? Am I really so ugly that you must sneak around to see pictures of other women?

Another aspect of this is the realization that her husband has a fantasy life going on that she has known nothing about. After getting through the shock of her first discovery, Cassandra found that more pain still awaited her. This came about when she read the following portion of my husband's book, *At the Altar of Sexual Idolatry.*

For the man given over to sexual sin, this imaginary life revolves almost exclusively around sex, and in his sexual fantasy world everything always transpires just the way he imagines it. The girl (or guy) in the fantasy is extremely attractive. She acts exactly as he wants, and her only wish is to satisfy his every desire. The girl's features can be changed in an instant. One moment she is a tall blonde. A few minutes later she becomes an exotic girl from Oriental descent. Perhaps later she is a vivacious girl from African heritage. The variations are as numerous as the world's female population itself. Not only can the partner be changed instantly, so, too, can the scenario. It may be the girl that he saw at the store that day "coming on to him." Later, it is his own personal harem. Again, the possibilities are endless.

In a man's world of imagination, everything is perfect. He does not have to deal with rejection. These dream girls all love him; none refuse to be with him. He never has to deal with impotence or nervousness either; everything goes smoothly. The girl is always flawless. There are no obnoxious odors, menstrual periods, diseases, or lack of interest. She does not act rudely, and she is not critical of him. She is not looking to take advantage of him or get his money. She will be willing to perform any desired sexual act because she exists solely to serve him. Finally, he does not need to worry about being caught by his wife or arrested by the authorities. In his perfect little dream world, nothing ever goes wrong.[1]

It was another painful blow to think that not even their times of intimacy were sacred; the raunchy thoughts were even carried into the bedroom. She again describes how she felt:

All this time I thought the vibrancy of our love-life was an expression of our love for each other, but now I realized that his excitement had been fueled by the filthy images he had seen on his favorite websites.

He had crass, carnal blinders on his eyes. Rather than looking through eyes of love he had trained his eyes in the art of lust. While he was with me physically, in his mind he had been with fifty other women. When he was touching me, he was imagining the body of someone else.

The pain of rejection for the wife goes very deep and is terribly hard to live with. Facing the unspoken (or sometimes even spoken) accusation that there is something wrong with her is like a slap in the face. So much of our value as women comes from our husband's admiration and love. To know he is longingly, yearningly looking at the faces and bodies of other women is a blow to the heart and soul like nothing else. The reality of such a revelation is so huge in its proportions that it takes one's breath away.

THE SENSE OF LOST RESPECT

This final reaction to discovering a husband's secret sin particularly comes into play for those women who are attempting to fight for their marriages. The terrible revelation that her husband is involved in such disgusting behavior can greatly affect the way she views him. This loss of respect can be very dramatic for some women. Before her terrible discovery of his secret life she had looked up to him as the man of her dreams; now he is seen as somewhat despicable, cowardly and repulsive.

Women tend to look to the husband to be the strong one of the family, the one whom she can depend upon to exercise wise and stable leadership. Most women want to look up to their husbands. This becomes difficult when he becomes involved in shameful and degrading behavior. Such weakness and lack of self-control often provokes a sense of disdain in her heart toward him.

Unquestionably, it is a challenge to follow a man you don't respect. I have often said that losing respect for a man is worse, in a sense, than losing the feelings of love. It is very difficult to be devoted to a man you don't respect.

Claudia describes what she experienced when she found out that her husband had been looking at porn and going to strip clubs:

> There was a time that I had so much admiration for my husband. I saw him as being above every other man. But when I found out about his secret life, something died inside of me for Carl. I no longer saw him the same way. I found myself questioning his judgment on everything. He lost a great deal of credibility in my eyes. I now felt like I had to lean on myself rather than my husband. I realized he had never been the man I thought he was.

I felt as though he had stolen the lofty respect I had always held him in. I couldn't help but wonder how he could be so weak and flimsy inside that he was unable to uphold his own dignity. "Is he such a coward that he can't fight for what we have together? How could he be so spiritually spineless that he would do such degrading things?"

These thoughts plagued me for months as the both of us worked our way through this terrible addiction.

My own struggles with lost respect for Steve were intense. At first, I could not handle him touching me. Inside I was screaming, "keep your hands off of me!" as though some "dirty ole man" was pawing me. I couldn't believe in him anymore and that was probably the thing that was hardest for me. He had gone from being one I had respected and revered to one I despised and disdained. It was the glue, in a sense, that held us together; but now even that was gone.

When a wife loses respect for her husband, something so huge and vital in the marriage relationship is lost – she loses her desire to submit to him. It is very difficult for a marriage to survive when God's authority structure has been destroyed. My own story is proof that it doesn't have to end that way. Many of the wives I deal with do not understand the concept of fighting for their marriages in the face of these overwhelming obstacles. Once they lost their respect for their husbands, they lost the will to fight for their marriages.

These are just a few of the true-to-life struggles a wife experiences when she first discovers her husband's problem. I have laid them out in this chapter knowing that you have probably already faced them yourself.

As you read this book you very well may find yourself facing numerous emotions. Some of the painful memories that it will bring up may discourage or even depress you. I want to encourage you to fight through and finish the book. Although this subject is a very heavy one and you may only be able to read a bit at a time, I want to encourage you to finish this race. Whatever may ultimately happen with your marriage, God wants to bring something very precious and wonderful into your life through the process.

I know from personal experience the good that can come from going through something so incredibly painful. When I was in the midst of overwhelming grief, Jesus came into my life in a powerful way. Although the pain didn't go away, it did somehow magnify the greatness of the love of God toward me. The very thing that I thought would destroy me became the means by which God extended to me an abundant life in Himself. I am grateful, so very grateful, that the Lord spared no expense to give me more of what I needed: Jesus. He used the hurt, the pain, the misery—all of it—to bring this about. I hope you too will experience this same thing in the days ahead.

2

THE PERFECT MARRIAGE

*"O Lord, teach me your perspectives
on marriage."*

I would say that most women enter marriage with a little bit of fairytale in them. I know I did! When I got married the first time (at the ripe old age of sixteen) there was that illusion in my heart that it was all about me. Even though I wasn't thinking in terms of a huge wedding, expensive gown and tons of flowers, still, in my mind, this was *my* day and this was the beginning of a lifetime of *me* getting what I wanted. I don't think it ever once occurred to me to consider what my fiancé might need or want. I assumed that I was what he needed! The truth is we were both selfish teenagers and too full of ourselves for anything good to come out of that marriage. Looking back it isn't hard to see why it quickly fell apart.

In spite of that disaster, I quickly found myself in another relationship. By the time I married Steve I had "matured" enough to set my sights much higher. Steve was six years older than me which somehow encouraged the illusion that I was now entering a life of marital bliss where all my needs would finally be met. I even saw myself, at some level, giving him my total love. Of course, it goes without saying that in the back of my mind this devotion had strings attached.

I have come to realize that my experience was fairly typical of the way young women view marriage. It almost seems that girls have a built-in fantasy about marriage. The man of our dreams is nothing short of Prince Charming himself, who will sweep us off our feet, into a happily-ever-after life written by Walt Disney himself! I don't think many of us entered marriage with our feet firmly planted on terra firma, comprehending the very real hurdles that would be involved in living with another person. In the fantasy world we have clung to, we will face every trial hand-in-hand, hearts knit together as one. For some reason there is a heavy curtain over the realities of marriage; hope springs eternal for the new bride. The thought that there could be insurmountable problems in the marriage simply seems unfathomable to us. Indeed, the fact of the matter is we have not considered that this one we are giving our hearts to could actually be the one to devastate us the most. No, in our Cinderella story it is always an external enemy who threatens our happiness; never the one we love.

One young lady in particular (I'll call her Beth) who I ministered to had that "glazed" look in her eyes as she considered her upcoming wedding. When I attempted to bring her down to earth about the realities of marriage, she confidently declared, "I know it's going to be hard. I know we'll have problems." When I asked her what those problems would be, in her very naïve and innocent way, she breezed over several subjects that she had overheard discussed as potential "deal breakers" in marriage. It was obvious she knew nothing about the realities and hardships of marriage. All she knew is what she had "felt" and "desired" her entire young life. So deeply entrenched was this fairytale in her psyche that Beth seemed to think that she and her Prince Charming would be ready to hold marriage seminars on how to have a perfect marriage in three short months! I can assure you that what actually happened was far different.

To her utter shock, Beth discovered that her new husband's sole ambition in life was not the continuance of their courtship romance. She was so out of touch with the reality of her husband's expectations that she was practically devastated during those first few months. She was clueless to the fact that the romantic feelings he exhibited when they dated were driven by male hormones and that he held a painfully practical notion about married life.

Beth entered the relationship oblivious to the fact that a guy's mindset about it is very different from that of the girl. He wants a helpmate for his future plans, a mother to his children, a cook and maid, and more than anything else, a mate with whom to share his bed.

The truth is that from the earliest days of wedlock, the husband and wife are approaching the marriage union from completely different mindsets, motivations and expectations. This is why a great change comes over most men once the wedding night is over. He has accomplished his goal, he has satisfied his passions and now he is simply looking to settle into the stability of a home, regular meals, regular sex and a normal existence. Since he has already won his girl's heart, there is no longer any purpose to be gained by holding hands with her, buying her flowers and calling her every hour. We actually imagined this routine would continue on into married life. *What were we thinking?*

No matter how much we wish it were not so, men simply do not think like women think. We often (without realizing it) want men to be more like our girlfriends than like the creatures God created them to be. We imagine a husband who will be someone we can relate to on an emotional level; someone we can talk to for hours about all our "girl stuff." But men are just not wired like that. For instance, do you realize these poor creatures can only think one dimensionally? Women can easily have three or four things going on inside at any given time: we are true multi-taskers!

When you consider the enormous gap which exists between men and women, it's a wonder any marriage makes it!

DISASTER JUST AHEAD

Yes, it doesn't take the typical new wife long to come out of the clouds into the mundane reality that she has just committed herself to spending the rest of her life tied to an emotional lughead! Not all men fit this characterization, but plenty do. Some women handle this disappointment with more grace than others. And I suppose it goes without saying that the greater a woman's expectations going into marriage, the greater the disappointment she is sure to face. If she can recover from her disillusionment quickly, the marriage will probably be spared a great deal of unnecessary tension.

Yet nothing can prepare a woman for the discovery that her husband is obsessed with the idea of having sex with other people. None of us (and I do mean *none*) expect to marry an unfaithful husband. With all of the other conflicts and disagreements we will have to work through in life we surely never thought that infidelity would be one of them. Little girl fantasies aside, there is nothing wrong with a woman entering this new life expecting the best and believing for the best. What woman would enter a marriage knowing that she can only expect the worst?

The trauma a woman feels when his illicit behavior is revealed is nothing less than earthshattering to her. She would have never expected him to be such a completely different person than the man he represented himself to be. To act like he was so in love with her and at the same time be so capable of giving himself away to others is beyond her ability to comprehend. She would have never considered in her wildest dreams that the man she would marry would be addicted to porn or something even worse.

Be that as it may, there is no getting around the fact that most husbands and wives came to the marriage bargaining-table with wrong ideas and hopes about marriage. Each had their own notion about what this union was going to look like—and boy were their ideas ever different!

So here you sit, realizing that you had unrealistic expectations of marriage and of your husband and unsure about what to do with the wreckage of your marriage. Did it end up this way as divine punishment because you didn't have all your spiritual ducks lined up? Was it because you had unrealistic expectations? No, God is not punishing you because you didn't do everything perfectly. You are in a very real sense a victim and God can completely relate to what you feel. He went through the same type of rejection and pain. He too knows what it's like to have the one He loves desire others more than Himself. He too has felt the pain of abandonment and betrayal.

So, if you are sitting on a pile of ashes that were once your dreams of the perfect marriage, now might be a good time to re-evaluate from God's perspective what marriage is supposed to be.

GOD'S TAKE ON THE PERFECT MARRIAGE

If we sincerely want God's best for our marriage, then we must turn to His Word. Let's start our quest by going all the way back to the beginning. The book of Genesis is where the institution of marriage was established. You all know the story, but I think it would be good to take a fresh look at that beginning.

God created Adam and assigned him to act as His designated authority over His entire creation. "Then the Lord God said, 'It is not good for the man to be alone; I will make him a helper suitable for him.'" (Genesis 2:18)

The Lord anesthetized Adam, extracted one of his ribs and used it as the material from which he fashioned Eve. Earth's first man woke up from his divinely induced stupor to find the perfect complement and helpmate to his lonely life.

There's no question that woman was a gift from the heart of God to man. The Genesis account tells us that God's express purpose in creating woman in the first place was so that she could be a helper to her husband. According to Strong's Dictionary, the root word for "helper" (Heb. *azar*) means: "to *surround*, that is, *protect* or *aid*: - help, succor." Thus, its derivative (Heb. *ezer*) used in Genesis 2 to describe a woman, would mean that she is there to act as his assistant—even as his protector!

So we can see that the Father's purpose in giving this beautiful creature to Adam was for her to act as a counterpart. She was made to care for him. She was not created as his inferior or his superior; she is the finishing touch on God's creation of man: his perfect complement.

And whether men want to acknowledge it or not, a woman is a force to be reckoned with! She can cook, clean, parent, build, earn wages, organize and manage a home. When a woman is operating in the capacity with which God created her there is nothing that can stop her! I mean, she can make a dungeon a palace; she can turn a desert into a paradise! Her qualities are far and wide! No wonder Solomon exclaimed, "He who finds a wife finds a good thing and obtains favor from the Lord." (Proverbs 18:22)

Adam and Eve had the closest thing to the perfect marriage that this earth would ever see. Adam possessed the perfect balance of strength and sensitivity, dignity and vulnerability, leadership and humility. As the head of the family, he was Eve's provider, defender and close companion. Adam truly was her Prince Charming and they really did enjoy the fairytale marriage.

Unfortunately, the beautiful marital union which God created in the Garden has, in large part, been degraded over time. This terrible deterioration began when Eve stepped outside of her proper place of submission and listened to the serpent (1 Timothy 2:14) and as Adam stepped out of his proper place of authority and allowed his wife to lead.

The process of death entered mankind and spoiled everything it touched—including marriage. Men and women have both been corrupted by sin, pride and selfishness ever since.

Consider the husband's responsibility in this relationship, for instance. Paul gave husbands an unequivocal command when he said, "Husbands, love your wives, just as Christ also loved the church and gave Himself up for her." (Ephesians 5:25) This is a powerful statement! How did Christ love the Church? He gave everything He had to give for her—including His life. She was the apple of His eye. Isn't that what the fairytale is? Isn't that what we wanted? Isn't that the kind of husband we signed up for? What could be wrong with wanting a husband who treated us like that?

Well, there is nothing wrong with desiring the perfect husband and the perfect marriage as long as we are willing to become the perfect wife. The only husband who can love us like Christ loved the church is one who is utterly consecrated to God. But even if you had such a husband, unless you are willing to live with that same level of consecration, your marriage will still be riddled with problems.

We can't have a perfect marriage in this sin-stained world, but we can have one that is near perfect—if we are willing to return to the pattern that was lived out in the Garden. You see, Adam and Eve lived in unbroken fellowship with God. Apparently it was normal fare for the Lord to "walk in the Garden" with them. (Genesis 3:8)

They lived in sight of "the beauty of His holiness." (Psalm 29:2 KJV) He was the great Center of everything that made up their lives. And when two people live with God truly as the center of their lives and relationship, their marriage will become as close to perfect as can be found today.

PROBLEMS IN PARADISE

One of the most amazing things I have seen is when a man gets right with God at Pure Life Ministries and returns home to a wife who is actually disappointed in the change. I know it sounds crazy, but I have witnessed this many times over the years. The husband experiences true repentance, changes his life, gives God the preeminent position in his heart, allows the Lord to begin correcting every fault and sin in his life and starts down the road to consecrated living. When he arrives back in the home after being in the Residential Program for nine months he truly is a new creature in Christ! He now loves his wife and is patient with the kids. He spends time in prayer and the Word every morning. He wants to be in church every time the doors are open. In short, he is everything she ever dreamed of having! Or so she thought.

So why would she be disappointed in such a change as this? Because she didn't consider what it would mean to her life to be married to such a man. If he has made God first in his life, there is an expectation of her to do the same. For instance, if he quits watching carnal television, how could she continue watching it? If he gets up early to spend time with God, how could she stay in bed? You see, the perfect marriage requires both partners to give themselves utterly to God.

Yes, there truly is a fairytale marriage to be had by any child of God—I know because I have one. Steve and I both had to separate ourselves from the things of this world; we both had to let God correct us and humble us; we both had to renounce every form of self-will. Well, I think you get the picture.

So what am I saying here? Should you give up on your fantasy of a fairytale marriage? Absolutely not! You simply must give up on the notion that the husband is the only one who must change to bring it about. Both must change; both must sacrifice; both must seek God with all their hearts.

The only way the fairytale marriage is going to happen is to put God in the center of it. He must have the supreme place in your lives. I realize that your husband's sexual sin has been an unfair betrayal, but there is much more to having a fulfilling marriage than the absence of unfaithfulness. If you and your husband don't allow God to have His rightful place in your lives, your marriage will always be a contest between two sinful people each trying to have their own way—even if it comes at the expense of the other.

3

WHERE IS GOD IN ALL THIS?

"O Lord, help me to see Your hand in this crisis."

I don't think I will ever forget the day that Steve dropped the bomb on me! An atomic explosion ripped through my life with such force, it literally took me weeks to realize what had happened. Actually, I don't think I was ever really able to comprehend my new reality. I had to learn to live with the fact that my husband was more in love with illicit sex than he was with me.

As the dust settled, I began to see our relationship in a new light. Prior to his great confession—that he had been involved with pornography and prostitutes during our entire two-year marriage—I had been forced to deal with a hodge-podge of unexplainable actions and behavior. Now a puzzle was coming together in my mind. Stray fragments of unanswered questions began to fit into a composite of a person I had not known up until this moment. I started to make sense out of all those nagging little mysteries. From the outset, I had been blaming myself for the problems in our marriage. I was "out of it" and just didn't understand my husband. Now it became clear that it wasn't me who was to blame. All those times I thought I was losing my mind because I couldn't make sense out of the explanations he would offer over some of his behaviors were actually tell-tale signs that he had another existence he kept hidden from me.

I had a number of issues I had to work through. I made a lot of mistakes in those early days and one of the biggest was my perspective of God's role in the whole business. To be honest, I think I was looking for someone to pin all the blame on. God was the most available and obvious recipient.

"So God," I demanded; "You knew what was in this man; why did You allow me to get into this disastrous marriage in the first place? You could have shown me what a disaster it would be. Surely You could have stopped me from going through with this marriage, right? Why are You letting him destroy me like this? What possible good could come from any of this? I'm humiliated, ashamed, hurt, broken; I have no hope for future happiness. Why didn't You intervene?" I think you get the idea about the questions I posed to the Lord. Maybe you've asked the same sort of things.

The Lord didn't answer those questions right away. I had to go through many painful experiences before I could handle the truth about why the Lord allowed all of this to happen. I could never have imagined the answer I eventually received. But what I learned through it was that most women who find themselves in this situation are there because God is doing something far more important and deeper than just giving us what we want; He is using it to give us what we need.

PRE-MARITAL LIFESTYLE

Many women set themselves up for tragedy because they have developed a wrong attitude about God's role in their lives. Perhaps I could say that they are charter members of the Bless-My-Wonderful-Plans club. As we talked about in the last chapter, they entered holy matrimony in a Pollyanna mindset. They viewed their husband and their dream of marriage to him through bright, rose-colored glasses. In other words, they were imposing on him their fantasy of Prince Charming. They were all too ready to believe the very best about him—not in a spirit of *agape* love but in sheer naiveté. Had God written a message in the sky, "You're about to make a huge mistake!" they would have looked the other way and acted like they didn't see it. They believed what they wanted to believe.

Then the terrible day of discovery came when they found out the truth about their husbands. Not only was he not the Prince Charming they had imagined him to be, but as far as they were concerned he was a downright deviant!

Their first reaction toward the Lord is that He had failed them. This thought opens the door to a cascade of questions like those I asked: "Lord, how could you let this happen to me?!!!"

One of the great revelations I eventually learned was that such questions were perilously close to becoming accusations against God—dangerous stuff if not kept in check. Such charges are based upon the false premise that marriage is supposed to be the key to a woman's happiness and wellbeing. And if we are not careful we begin to wander into the carnal mindset that somehow God has failed us. After all, He is God; He is sovereign and should make everything near perfect in our lives.

Joyce's story is so typical of this kind of thinking. I knew her well and can still remember what her life was like before she met Rick thirty years ago. She was divorced from her third husband and living happily as a single woman. She had just come back to the Lord and had really gotten her life together. For the first time since I had known her she didn't feel like she had to have a man to be complete in life. She was no longer looking for that elusive relationship that would be the answer to all her dreams. She was in love with Jesus and He repaid her devotion by helping her get her life in order: a nice apartment close to her job, a decent car and all the fixins for a pleasant life as a single woman. Her faith was alive and vibrant. She spent time with the Lord every morning and much of her time at home was spent doing Bible studies or listening to worship music. She was such an inspiration to Steve and me. Her life epitomized Christian contentment.

And then one day, and I mean in one day, everything changed. She had been attending the singles group at her church every Friday night when Mr. Wonderful suddenly appeared. Rick was a brand new Christian, fresh out of a stint in jail and there was Joyce, perky, pretty and ready to help. There was an instant chemistry between the two and in less than a month they were married.

What is wrong with this picture? In fewer than thirty days this woman decided that she was prepared to spend the rest of her life with this man! What followed were many years of misery—a lousy marriage that continues to be so to this day. And, of course, once she discovered what he was really like, the accusations against God began to spew out.

What happened to Joyce? If she was living a life so pleasing to God, why did He allow this to happen to her? There's no question that she was doing many things right, but she also had a strong will that had never been dealt with. There was a part of her that wanted to please the Lord, but the idol of men was still lurking inside her. When it came right down to it, she walked away from God in her heart to have what she wanted.

Joyce's foolishness to marry a man on such short notice may be an extreme example, but it still points to this mentality that God is obligated to bless our plans. It should go without saying that He is under no such obligation. Rather, it is our responsibility to painstakingly seek Him until we are absolutely certain we know His will and then to follow it carefully and obediently, even fearfully.

Rather than blasting God with a slew of accusatory questions regarding our plight, allow me to ask women like Joyce a few questions of my own. How much time did you spend seeking

God about His will regarding this relationship? Considering the lifelong implications involved in the decision to marry this man, were you absolutely positive you heard Him tell you to move forward with it? Were you so committed to obeying His will and purpose for your life that you were prepared to walk away from this relationship? Was your mindset one of following God's will or one of going your own way with the expectation that He would be required to bless your will?

One of the great tragedies about painful marriages is that many of them could have easily been avoided. There is no question about it: the safest place to be in life is in the center of God's will. The only way a person can be assured of that place of safety is to learn to walk meekly before God in every way.

Christians who live for themselves and expect God to bless their lives are living in dangerous presumption. Many women whom I have dealt with over the years entered disastrous marriages simply because they did not know what it means to really trust the Lord. They entered marriage with a rather casual presumption that everything would turn out well and that somehow their love would get them through. Women with this attitude are also quick to jump ship at the first sign of trouble.

THIS WAS GOD'S WILL? MAYBE!

Many women I have dealt with over the years (and I include myself in this group) were actually doing God's will when they decided to marry their husbands—even though they weren't "painstakingly" seeking it! In my case, I actually went against my pastor's counsel to marry Steve. As it turned out, our marriage was actually part of the Lord's plan for our lives—but I sure can't take any credit for it! I was one of the fortunate ones who blundered into what eventually turned out to be a great marriage.

I have the benefit of looking back over years of wonderful ministry to others as evidence that our marriage was indeed part of God's purpose for my life. Other women don't have that assurance.

Then there are those women who really were living godly lives when they met their husbands-to-be. They tried to respond to the exciting possibility in the right way and everything pointed to the Lord giving the green light.

That describes Karla's situation in 1995. She was 33-years old and expecting to be single the rest of her life when she met Ed. Common interest in the Lord seemed to draw the two together, so, after dating for almost two years, they got married in September of 1997. Before long they were both hired at the Teen Challenge farm in Rehrersburg, PA: Ed as a counselor and Karla as an accountant. It seemed as though they would live "happily ever after."

However, within a few months, she began to notice changes in Ed's moods. He would often go into periods of withdrawal, not saying a word, and just barely responding to any attempt she would make at having a conversation with him. But perhaps the problem that puzzled Karla more than anything was the absence of romance and physical affection in their relationship. She wanted his love and affection so badly, but it seemed like the more she asked for it, the more he refused. As much as she tried, she just couldn't understand what was happening. It hurt so much that she would often cry all night long because she felt so unwanted. The only thing she could conclude was that she was so unattractive that even her husband didn't want her.

When they had been married almost a year, Ed finally confessed to Karla that he had been involved in homosexual relationships with young men before their marriage. He also told her that he was masturbating on a regular basis. She felt betrayed and angry that he had not been honest with her about something as important as this. But she tried her best to put this discovery—and all of the fears that came with it—behind her and make the best of their marriage. Over the next several years, they both presented the picture of a happy marriage to family and friends. The truth was that there was no intimacy in their marriage and little connection between them emotionally.

One day, Ed confessed to her that he had been involved homosexually with a young man he had met at work. Weeks of bitter anguish followed for Karla. This new hurt went to depths she had never experienced before.

Ed resigned his position as a counselor and, with nowhere else to turn, reluctantly entered the Pure Life Ministries Residential Program on May 14, 2004. About six weeks later, she received a letter from Ed asking her to forgive him, not just for his sexual sin, but also for the pride, the selfishness and the lack of love he had shown. Tears streamed down her face, because she knew that for the first time in their marriage Ed was really beginning to understand how much he had hurt her.

The first time Karla visited Ed at the Pure Life campus, she immediately noticed that his attitude was different. He was much more open with her about things than he had ever been before and talked freely about what God had been teaching him. He was more humble and more concerned about her and did whatever he could to make sure she was comfortable and well taken care of. He took the initiative to pray with her, and, one night, as they were walking, he took her hand and held it in his. It had been six years since he had done that! Ed graduated from the PLM Residential Program on November 14, 2004.

Once he returned home, it was clear that the change was real and would be long lasting. For instance, for the first time since they had been married they began spending time in prayer together. Perhaps even more indicative of the new man her husband had become, Ed started showing sincere affection to her.

In 2005, Ed and Karla were invited to return to Pure Life Ministries as interns. Today, Ed is an ordained pastor and is director of the Residential Program. Karla is the organization's accountant. Yes, there was a time when it would have been difficult to believe that she hadn't made a terrible mistake in marrying Ed Buch, but now she can see how God has used her pain to do a deep work inside her and to use their redeemed marriage for His glory.

THE GOOD GOD WANTS TO BRING OUT OF THIS

Whether or not it was actually God's will for you to marry your husband, the fact remains that you have entered into a covenant relationship with him before God. You must now take care to find God's will and obey it.* The worst thing you could do would be to make matters worse for yourself by turning away from the Lord in favor of the easiest option.

I realize that when you are being victimized by someone it is very easy to justify doing whatever it takes to protect yourself. One of the best biblical examples of this sort of thing is what happened to Joseph.

He must have been terrified when his brothers sold him to a traveling caravan of Ishmaelites! "What will happen to me? Where is God in all of this? What have I ever done to deserve such treatment?" Joseph had every human reason to question God's goodness when this tragedy came upon him. Nevertheless, when he was sold to the captain of the Pharaoh's bodyguard, he did his utmost to obey the man and keep his heart right with the Lord.

All was going well until Potiphar's wife began her campaign of seduction and then, when he rejected her advances, accused him of attempting to rape her! He was subsequently thrown into an Egyptian prison. Yet, once again, he responded with an incredible determination to please the Lord with his life. Of course, eventually he was vindicated and exalted to the right hand of the Pharaoh himself. What is often lost in this story is that the greatest blessing was not that he was given a position

---

* We will talk about whether or not divorce is an option in a later chapter.

of power. The important thing that happened was the way the Lord purged the self-righteousness out of Joseph that had kept him from really knowing Him. Truly, what his brothers meant for evil, God meant for good! (Genesis 50:20) The riches of Egypt went by the wayside thousands of years ago, but what God did inside that dear man is his to enjoy forever.

Job, Abraham, Daniel, Paul and many others have suffered similar experiences, but you can see in their lives who they were trusting in. The Lord put them on a path—painful as it was—that led them to Himself. In the midst of all of the crushings, anxieties, and persecutions, He was quietly bringing about the fragrance of Christ in their lives. Coming into the life of Jesus Christ and being conformed to His image is a strong desire within every true believer.

Now consider your dilemma. You're in the storm of your life and you're asking what good could possibly come of it. I can tell you from experience that through the immense pain you are experiencing right now, God is doing something deep and powerful inside you that you, too, will possess in eternity. This is no fantasy—it is real. You only must embrace God's will and His dealings with you in the midst of it all and He will bring untold blessings into your life through it.

4

CONTRIBUTING FACTORS

BY STEVE GALLAGHER

*"O Lord, help me to better understand
my husband's struggle."*

I have been recruited by my wife to contribute to this book in the hopes I can provide you with some background about your husband's struggle. Having dealt with this issue in my own life and having ministered to thousands of sexual addicts over the past three decades, I have a fairly good comprehension of how the enemy has used sexual sin to destroy men's lives. If I can help you to step back and see beyond your husband's situation—to view the big picture of what is happening to millions of American men in our day—my hope is that it will actually diminish the sting of betrayal; the deep hurt of feeling so personally rejected as a woman.

In a sense, it probably doesn't matter to you that millions of other women have experienced the same thing you are going through now. And yet, it *does* matter. When a woman is smacked in the face with the sudden revelation that her husband is obsessed with the idea of having sex with other people, it is very normal for her to become engulfed in her own crisis. Her husband, her marriage, her feelings suddenly take on enormous proportions. Of course, this response is to be expected. Nevertheless, the more the wife focuses on it the more painful it becomes.

The point of this chapter isn't to minimize his sinful, selfish actions or the very real suffering you have experienced because of it. My hope is that when you come to a fuller understanding of how the enemy lured your husband down this road—many, many years ago—you will be able to see the situation less subjectively; you will have a profound revelation that will sink deeply into your heart: "My husband had this problem long before he ever knew me and it has nothing whatsoever to do with my femininity, the shape of my body, what we do in bed or anything else about me. This is *his* problem and always has been." Furthermore, his sexual sin was never meant to actually be the way it has felt to you: as a personal attack against you as a person.

If I can shed light on sexual addiction, I believe some of the questions you have grappled with will be answered for you. In the hopes of at least helping to diminish this sense of personal rejection and to give you a better idea of how he became the man he is, I want to take you back to his childhood.

THE DEVELOPMENT OF SEXUAL ADDICTION

Sexual addicts aren't born, they are made. Your husband is not obsessed with sexual pleasure because he was born with an excessive "libido." He did not come into this world as some sort of mentally deformed freak. What happened to him is not much different than what millions of other men have experienced.*

The first thing to understand is that sexual addiction is primarily a spiritual problem.† His problems began as a lust for sexual sin. As he indulged in it, the sin gradually grew into a massive form of demonic bondage.

---

* It is also is an age-old problem. In fact, illicit sex was the main drawing power of the fertility cults that the enemy so effectively used to lure God's people away from Him in Old Testament times.
† Please don't allow your husband to go down the path of attributing it all to emotional problems that stemmed from not receiving proper parenting as a child. His only hope of change is found in the repentance that comes from taking complete responsibility for his actions, not in blaming his parents—or anyone else for that matter.

Let me put it this way (at the risk of sounding cliché-ish): his current problems are a direct result of the inter-workings of "the world, the flesh and the devil" in his life over the years. These three "entities" have worked hand-in-hand to allow something that began as boyhood curiosity to grow into the monster it eventually became. Let's take a look at your husband's past in regard to their influence on him.

THE FLESH

Human beings were created with certain innate drives, impulses, and appetites such as hunger, thirst, and even the desire for sex. There is nothing wrong with sex as long as it is confined to intimacy between a man and his wife. God wants married couples, whom He has enjoined, to enjoy each other—thus, He made it a pleasurable experience. However, confusion and perversion emerge when people deviate from the purpose for which God ordained sex.

We all know that men and women differ in their sexual drives. Generally speaking, men are much more driven by sexual desire than women. Women enjoy sex too, but their passions are nearly always tied to their desire to receive acceptance from and an emotional attachment with their partner. Men tend to be driven by the same kind of sexual craving that is inherent in the male gender of nearly any animal species—hormonal pleasure.

This animalistic desire begins for the typical male when the strange new sensations of puberty begin to well up within him. Before long he discovers that it is very pleasurable to touch himself "down there." At some point, he does this to the point of bringing himself to ejaculation—an electrifying experience for a youngster. It isn't difficult to understand why most teenage boys develop habits of masturbation from a very early age.

The youngster doesn't understand what is occurring in his body or in his life. He doesn't realize that the reason this new experience is so captivating is that he has a fallen nature that is drawn to sin. "The flesh," as the Bible calls it, has no concern with pleasing God. It is only interested in comfort, pleasure, and the preservation of self. The flesh longs for gratification at any cost. It always seeks that which is sensual and satisfying. God, family and others take a secondary position to personal interests. It only wants its lusts and desires to be fully satisfied.

The young man doesn't understand that his indulgence in masturbation is allowing a very powerful habit to form in his life. This habit will eventually form a lifestyle. Deep ruts are being dug into his life through repeated behavior. Responding to sexual urges becomes second nature to him.

Typically, by the time he becomes a believer, the passions of the flesh have already ruled his life for many years. These deeply entrenched habits have been constantly reinforced and strengthened by the old nature which has become accustomed to having its own way. It is true that when he is born again, the Spirit of God now indwelling him will nudge him away from sin and toward holiness. Nevertheless, the flesh is still a powerful, dominating force. Comparatively, at this early stage, the spirit is an underfed weakling!

Not only must he deal with a powerful, hormonally-driven passion, a habit of masturbation that has become entrenched in his life, a soul that has been increasingly twisted by sin, but he soon comes to realize that the culture in which he lives is permeated with a host of allurements to tantalize him!

THE WORLD

In one sense, men involved in pornography and sexual sin are simply by-products of the world in which they live. An immoral mindset has gripped America—indeed, the entire Western Civilization. We have slipped far away from the decency that once established acceptable standards for our nation. That morality is now openly scoffed as prudish and old-fashioned. Lewd conduct is now the norm.

Everywhere one turns, he finds the promotion and exploitation of sex. Hollywood is committed to portraying the hero as the master seducer. Movies are overrun with beautiful, scantily clad (or nude) starlets. Advertisers blatantly use sex to sell their products. Fashion designers do their utmost to make sure that young women show off as much flesh as possible. Company parties hire male or female strippers for entertainment. Homosexuality is unashamedly flaunted and advocated. People openly live together in sin. Needless to say, the moral fabric of our society is being unraveled right before our eyes.

Society teaches young people that illicit sex is not only accepted, but expected. Take the daily life of an average fourteen-year old boy. While he's waiting for his younger sister to get ready for school, he checks out YouTube and catches some of the latest videos, most of them filled with plenty of innuendo and skin. Later that morning his health class teacher refuses to take a moral stand against pre-marital sex or even homosexuality, and a text message from a girl who thinks he is cute casually lets him know her parents will not be home tomorrow night. While he walks down the hallway he overhears the popular, and often precocious, boys talking about their sexual escapades in between their sexually charged assessments of the girls passing by.

On the way home from school, he stops at a friend's house where they cruise the latest Facebook pics and posts from their "friends," hoping some of the girls they are looking to hook up with have responded. A few hours later, he is home and in front of the TV, where the characters of his favorite shows regularly engage in various sexual scenarios. The hero—the "Casanova" type—is almost always hooking up with someone. Then there are the commercials that showcase beautiful women selling anything and everything imaginable. When his sister isn't looking, he scans her stack of *Cosmo Girl* and *Seventeen* magazines drinking in the seductive advertisements and latest answers to the questions about sex posted by the readers. After everyone else has gone to bed, he enters the vast, dark realm of internet gaming sites, where links to X-rated websites are prominently displayed.

With such overwhelming exposure as this, why should anyone be surprised that a young teenager turns into a sex addict? Especially considering that "teens spend an average of four to six hours per day interacting with the mass media in various forms."[1] And a recent study by the Kaiser Family Foundation found that the typical teenager "...will view nearly 14,000 sexual references per year" on television.[2]

As if this overwhelming influence isn't enough for a youngster to deal with, he must also deal with a culture that has become increasingly friendly toward pornography. The internet has made every form of perversion accessible to whoever has access to it.

A permissive society, such as ours, makes the road to sexual addiction very smooth. Just as our culture makes it easy for a person to slide down the path deeper and deeper into bondage, it also makes it equally difficult for the person, who so desires, to escape it. Everywhere he turns, he is constantly confronted with and reminded of what he is trying to avoid.

If your husband is less than sixty years of age, he has grown up in a sexually saturated culture. When he became a Christian, he came to understand that it was wrong, but you must understand that everything around—everything!— tells him otherwise. The collective mindset of our society is extremely powerful in its ability to form our attitudes. This is certainly true regarding sexuality.

Not only must your husband deal with the powerful urges of a male and the influences of our culture, but there is also a host of spiritual enemies at hand to keep him locked into his burgeoning addiction.

THE DEVIL

There is a sophisticated army of beings who operate under the auspices of the devil himself. This spiritual organization is composed of demons of various sizes, strengths, abilities and functions. (c.f. Luke 11:14; Matthew 12:22; 1 John 4:6) They range from princes of countries (Daniel 10:13) down to lowly soldiers. (Luke 8:30) Paul gives an indication of this intricate hierarchy in the Book of Ephesians, "For our struggle is not against flesh and blood, but against the rulers, against the powers, against the world forces of this darkness, against the spiritual forces of wickedness in the heavenly places." (Ephesians 6:12)

Like any military outfit, it seems as though there are generals, captains, and soldiers—or at least some equivalent thereof—and that demons have been specially assigned to harass and attack individuals. This is mostly conjecture of course, but apparently the designated demon will be selected on the basis of that person's particular area of struggle. To the one who struggles with depression, a devil of dark gloom would be appointed. For those who battle a hot temper, a spirit of rage or murder would be given the task; and for an exaggerated sex drive, an unclean spirit would be commissioned. It is likely that these demons have the ability to create spiritual atmospheres which are conducive to an individual's struggle.

With that in mind, let's return to his childhood one more time. As we have seen, powerful physical urges began to assert themselves when he entered puberty. When he became conscious of his sexuality as an adolescent, there was undoubtedly some foul spirit on hand to lure him down the path of sexual addiction. It was there to draw attention to some form of temptation; it was there to remind him of past pleasurable experiences; and it was there to emphasize the shame of his secret sin—to encourage him to keep it hidden from others.

THE MAN YOU MARRIED

For many years this spiritual bondage became more entrenched in your husband's life. The real sense of pleasure from it was gone long ago. Like a junkie who can't remember *ever* enjoying a fix, he has continued on his course because the compulsion to do so is very powerful inside him.

Now allow me to address some questions that most wives ask in this situation. Let's take them one at a time.

"How could my husband be involved in such foul perversion?" Let's face it: sexual perversion has become the norm in our fallen culture. As I have already shown, your husband has gone down the same path millions of other hapless victims of the devil have traveled.

"What is wrong with me that makes me so unsatisfying to him?" Your husband has been trained from childhood to think of sex as being something carnal and dirty. It goes without saying that pornography has only deepened this perspective. The truth is that it wouldn't matter how perfect you looked or what you did in bed: as long as sexual addiction has its grip on his heart, it will not be possible for him to be satisfied with a normal sex life. However, I can tell you from personal experience that this will be increasingly less true of him as he goes through the process of repentance.

"Why did he hide his struggles from me when we were courting?" Because of the shame associated with masturbation and sexual sin, your husband has been hiding his behavior all of his life. I don't mean to justify his dishonesty. The right thing would have been for him to confess his struggles before asking you to marry him. However, it is possible that he honestly believed that his issues with sexual sin would come to an end on your wedding night. This is a very common fallacy among single sex addicts.

"Why has he become so cold and distant with me?" Emotional aloofness is one of the terrible consequences to being given over

to blatant sin of any kind. I realize it feels like more rejection, but, once again, it really has nothing to do with you. This is a common characteristic of *all* sinners.

I hope that seeing your husband's sin in light of what others experience has helped to lessen the sense of personal rejection for you. Now that we have addressed that struggle, I believe my wife has some things to share with you about your own life.

5

LEVEL PLAYING FIELD

*"O Lord, help me to see
my own need."*

There is a grave danger involved in the discovery that you are married to a sexual addict. No, the danger I'm talking about is not that you might lose your marriage or contract some deplorable STD. The peril I am referring to is how this painful news might affect you spiritually. The fact is that women have natures that are every bit as fallen as their husbands'. We all have the potential to become something very ugly and un-Christlike inside.

It is pretty difficult for most of us to wrap our minds around our own need to guard our hearts when we've been clobbered by the shocking reality of our husband's unfaithfulness. It's hard enough to digest the fact that one's husband is obsessed with the bodies of other people. Most wives could handle this news if that was all that was involved, but the fact of the matter is that there is an entire conglomeration of sins crowded together in his secret life.

The poor wife soon discovers that her husband's heart is eaten alive with a relentless, insatiable lust. Then she has to face the reality that he has been maintaining a personality that is completely different from the one she has known. On top of those distressing insights is the added burden of discovering the enormity of his duplicity. She doesn't know if she can believe *anything* he says! The only good thing that seems to come out of this horrible thing is that she can now see that she hasn't been imagining things. There is now an explanation for his aloofness, his sneakiness and his double-talk.

This news is a horrific blow and the woman's life has been turned upside down. Trust is shattered, intimacy is gone and life as she has known it is different. Then there is the unrelenting pain; waves of grief that keep rolling in, threatening to completely overwhelm her.

The exposure of her husband's secret sin becomes all consuming. In a strange twist, she becomes as obsessed with his secret life as he is. As she moves through the range of emotions involved in this discovery, one question keeps popping up in her mind: "How could he be so perverted, so deceitful?" The more she focuses on his behavior, the more disgusted she becomes with him.

She cannot relate to his fascination with sex. It seems so dirty, so disgraceful, so shameful. Her respect for him as a man plummets. She also has no point of reference whatsoever about his duplicitous lifestyle. "He is a liar; that's all there is to that!" She cannot imagine someone being so completely false.

It is at this point in the process that she becomes extremely vulnerable to the enemy. The devil will not be content with destroying one soul; he wants to ruin both of their lives. As the wife struggles with the confusion and the myriad emotions involved with this discovery, the enemy skillfully steps in and begins to offer suggestions that appeal to the woman's anger and also to her own pride. Of course, the thoughts he introduces to her mind are offered in first person—as if they were her own thoughts. "I would never do anything like that!"

The devil is unrelenting in his attacks. In the same way he has led her husband to think impure thoughts, he now coaxes the hurting wife with self-righteous thoughts. He is masterfully building into her mind an ugly attitude of superiority.

This creeping virus begins to make a home for itself within her heart. The more she recites to herself his sinful actions, the more sickened she becomes by him.

This is the place where a subtle shift in roles can happen—a phenomenon which typically goes undetected. So often, once the sin is out in the open, the husband will sort of cower under the guilt and shame associated with sexual sin. In her anger, the wife will often beat him down emotionally. In an attempt to prove to her that he truly is sorry about his actions, he will unknowingly hand over to her the spiritual headship of the home. In her mind, this is only right since he has disqualified himself to be in that position. None of this is spoken out loud; it is just an imperceptible changing of the guard, so to speak.

The hurting wife is simply responding to her husband from her own hurt feelings. I mean, it's not like she has thought everything through. For instance, she doesn't realize that when she compares her sins (which seem so insignificant) to his (which seem enormous), she is going right down the path the enemy has laid out for her. Nevertheless, the more she indulges herself in that thinking, the more deeply entrenched it becomes in her heart.

Let's face it, what wife, upon receiving such devastating news is going to rush to her prayer closet and cry out, "O God what evil is in me?" The typical reaction is pain, anger, disgust and feelings of being offended. This ruthless enemy, which plagues every believer, is right there to build a very prideful mindset upon these normal human reactions.

The wife's great need at this critical point is not to see the blackness of her husband's sin but to see her own danger. "What danger? I am not the one who has given over to sexual sin!" she might suggest with a certain degree of incredulity. Nevertheless, she is in great danger of losing sight of her own sinful condition and turning into a Pharisee. I know this seems a little out of left field to think this way, but I have been down this path not only in my own life but in many other women's lives. Believe me, it is of greater importance than you may realize.

One of our needs is to understand the truth about God and ourselves. Until we have looked ourselves squarely in the face and been gut-level honest about what dwells within us, we will live a fantasy about who we really are and will only have a superficial understanding about God's grace or even the need for it! Women's issues tend to be hidden heart issues: secret attitudes, wrong assumptions, high-mindedness and so on. The spiritual danger wives face in this kind of situation is that they can easily point at their husbands' glaring sin while theirs remains nicely tucked away in their hearts, unseen to human eyes.

One of the most effective lies the devil has promoted is that we are good people, devoted Christians. The typical attitude many wives have goes something like this: "Yeah, I have a few areas in my life that God is dealing with me on, but the Lord does not expect me to be so holy that I never fail and He surely wouldn't categorize my shortcomings along with my husband's complete failure."

One woman I dealt with quite a bit that had this attitude was Nancy. Those who know her would consider her to be a godly woman. She spends time with the Lord every morning. People know her as a warm friend, willing to do anything to help someone in need. And yet at home, where no one else sees her, she becomes someone altogether different. Her Christianity seems to be nonexistent when it comes to her husband.

Once Nancy found out about her husband's sexual sin, she unduly elevated her spiritual level far above his. She saw herself as godly and her husband as carnal. She became very hard on him, continually treating him with disdain.

Without realizing what she was doing, she was slowly

emasculating him; stripping him of any authority in her life. In fact, in her mind, he was less than a man now. As is always true of self-righteous people, she compared her strengths to his weaknesses. The more fixated she became on his failures, the more she rose up in ugly pride. And, of course, focusing on his shortcomings allowed her to completely disregard the sinful condition of her own heart.

One wise pastor we know once said, "Most people either come out of a life of deep sin or out of a life of deep self-righteousness." That is so true.

The ironic thing about Nancy's story is that her husband was responding to the Lord's correction. He sincerely repented of his sin and, in his own way, sought the Lord. True, his "form" of Christianity didn't match up to what she expected. Although his spiritual growth was slow, he really was maturing. In the meantime, Nancy's spiritual life was drying up.

It is this kind of haughty attitude that brings spiritual deterioration; that's why it's so important that we vigilantly guard against it! It is very dangerous for a woman to set herself up as the judge who can decide which sins are "bad" and which ones the Lord is willing to wink at. When we put ourselves in that position, we are basically claiming that we are right there on the same level with the Lord!

THE DANGER OF JUDGING OTHERS

I would like to invite you to carefully consider the following words written by a man who was full of the Spirit of God. He is commenting on the command Jesus gave, "Judge not, that ye be not judged. For with what judgment ye judge, ye shall be judged: and with what measure ye mete, it shall be measured to you again." (Matthew 7:1-2 KJV)

There are two kinds of judgment. One is of condemnation; the other is of mercy. The one is according to appearance and accusation of evil; the other is righteous judgment and according to truth and mercy. Jesus warns against the judgment which arises from faultfinding and condemning. The warning is this: you will be judged with your own judgment, and you will be measured with, or in your own measure. The measure which you use for others is the very same measure which will be used for you.

This is so serious a matter that it would seem as though all Christians would be overwhelmingly concerned over these words. But quite the contrary seems to be the fact. These words are quickly and easily forgotten by many. The reason is that the human heart is a judgment seat, before which everyone passes who is seen or thought of. All day long you are sitting as Judge in the court of your unseen heart. Unseen, that is, to men. Judging others—ceaselessly all day. Day by day, and sometimes by night. You are judging, judging, measuring everyone and everything. You do not always need full and sufficient evidence because you love yourself, and in that self love you think that you know. You judge by whims, and feelings, and fancies; by what you like and by what you do not like. You are the center. Your judgment is according to what people do or do not do in your favor—and for your glory—and for your satisfaction...

But now look at the other side of it. If you judge according to mercy, you will find that mercy increasing. As to your "measure," if you use on others the measure of mercy which God has used on you, then that mercy is what will be measured to you, and increasingly so. Look at the other side again. You will be judged with your own judgment, and shall be measured with your own measure. You will find that mercy is the only kind of judgment that you will want to bear, or be able to bear.[1]

These are frightening words! Jesus was accustomed to looking inside people's hearts. He could see the ugly, self-righteous attitude which the Pharisees fostered.

I can't help but think of the story in Luke 18 where Jesus shares about the Pharisee and the Tax Collector:

> And He also told this parable to some people who trusted in themselves that they were righteous, and viewed others with contempt: "Two men went up into the temple to pray, one a Pharisee and the other a tax collector. The Pharisee stood and was praying thus to himself: 'God, I thank You that I am not like other people: swindlers, unjust, adulterers, or even like this tax collector. I fast twice a week; I pay tithes of all that I get.'
>
> "But the tax collector, standing some distance away, was even unwilling to lift up his eyes to heaven, but was beating his breast, saying, 'God, be merciful to me, the sinner!' I tell you, this man went to his house justified rather than the other; for everyone who exalts himself will be humbled, but he who humbles himself will be exalted." (Luke 18:9-14)

I love this story because it reveals God's perspectives about people. The Pharisee compared himself to the sinful tax collector and thanked God he wasn't like that! And how similar is the self-righteous wife who might entertain the unspoken attitude: "Look at what a good life I lead, Lord. I do all the right things. You won't find any glaring sins in my life. I'm sure not like my sinful husband!" How many times I have seen the sinful husband humble himself before the Lord, in clear sight of his great need. Just like this publican, he can only see his own black heart and his need for forgiveness. The truth is that the longer you walk with the Lord the more you realize what a "tax collector" (i.e. sinful person) you really are.

Cassandra came into this revelation and it was liberating for her: "I knew that HE had a big problem. I knew that our marriage was a mess, but I mostly blamed him. I knew I wasn't spotless, but I was surely better than him. Oh, I was so blind. What I have learned thru (sic) this experience is that I was just as much a part of this tragedy as he was. I brought my pride and selfishness into this union just like he did. I controlled and manipulated just like he did and in the end I almost lost it all, just like he did. I was never any better than him. We are all wretched sinners, one no better than the next. Praise God for his amazing love and mercy!"

Cassandra had a spiritual breakthrough that has changed her life. Her attitude was typical of so many wives. Sure, we're willing to acknowledge our sinfulness in a general way, but if God begins to deal with us about our particular sins, we point at all we have been through as though it somehow justifies our behavior. The truth is we put Jesus on the cross every bit as much as any serial murderer, child molester or sex addict.

I heard an analogy about this human tendency to compare ourselves with others given many years ago. Imagine a world-class athlete on Santa Monica beach in Southern California. This man is incredibly strong and healthy. Standing next to him is a 75-year-old man. These two are about to engage in a contest. They must attempt to jump to Catalina Island, some twenty miles offshore. Obviously the athlete can jump a few feet further than the old man, but when you consider his effort in light of the distance, the difference is so insignificant it isn't even worth mentioning. I think that is a pretty clear picture about how God sees our sin.

I will never forget the time when God led me to sit down and make out a list of sins in my heart. My instructions were clear: "Write down everything in your heart that you don't want others to see." WOW! I was amazed at how ugly I was inside, how black my heart was. My tears were not shed over the grief of my sinful condition but from sheer embarrassment! I had been so deceived. I was so accustomed to looking at my spiritual life through rose-colored glasses. After all, there were no outward sins in my life; I spent two hours every day in devotions; I worked fulltime in the ministry; I had consecrated my life to the Lord. I considered myself to be a godly woman!

Now I realize that some believers are godlier than others. However, what I needed at that point was a serious attitude check! It was very painful to see what I was really like inside. But what came out of that list was much needed truth about how great my own need was. One sight of that long and dark list was enough to forever destroy the Pharisaical spirit I had been harboring. God didn't try to rub my nose in my faults, but He did use the whole situation to put me in my place.

Something else came out of that exercise: a brand new revelation about God's wonderful grace; yes, grace that was powerful enough to wash away the guilt and stain of sin. I came to realize that I will never be able to stand on my own merit. My only hope is what Jesus Christ accomplished for me and other sinners on Calvary.

When you come to face yourself, the playing field is leveled and you are now no longer a victim or a Pharisee, just a Christian who can live out the love of God to any sinner, including your husband. Of course the blow of his sin hurts and there is a terrible fracture in the relationship, but also coinciding with that broken-hearted pain is the common-ground understanding that one sinner has with another that can only result in compassion and the ability to stand with him through it.

6

FOUR UNHEALTHY
REACTIONS

*"O Lord, help me to react to this in a
godly way."*

Women who are married to men in sexual sin (or any
addictive lifestyle, for that matter) find themselves dealing
with issues in themselves they would have never had to face
in life if not for these circumstances. Over the years, I have
noticed that women tend to react to this terrible situation in
one of two ways. Those with strong personalities are inclined
to try to correct and control their husband's actions. Women
with more passive natures are likely to find ways to avoid
facing the hard facts about their husbands. The purpose of
this chapter is not to fault-find, but to help the hurting wife
come to recognize her natural reaction and how to better
handle it.

Of course, I realize that by presenting these natural
propensities, I run the risk of sounding too much like a textbook
or a machine. It goes without saying that people cannot always
be neatly plugged into preordained slots. Yet, I know from
much experience that women usually tend to be one way or the
other. In other words, it is in their "nature" to react a certain
way. But, as we shall see at the end of the chapter, God has a
way of responding that is found in *His* nature.

Before I move on, I want to briefly return to an issue I touched on in the opening sentence: that such women "find themselves dealing with issues in themselves they would have never had to face in life if not for these circumstances." I mean how many "normal" wives have to consider if they are enabling their husbands in some sinful way? How many "normal" wives feel like they have to restrain an out-of-control husband? The truth is that most wives don't feel a need to look over their shoulders through life and wonder if their husbands are up to no good. They are not forced to wrestle with suspicion and fear. They don't have to live in fear of the next "big confession." I think we all have to admit that this wife is subjected to problems that are anything but "normal."

Even if she had a fairytale mentality about marriage, she most likely understood she would face difficulties. But these problems are so off the path of what she thought she would face: you know, the usual stuff like how to raise kids, how to budget the finances, where to live and so on. Instead, she finds herself dealing with terms she could never have imagined: appeasing wife, police wife, enabling wife or bitter/angry wife. She is not only faced with all the consequences of a husband's unfaithfulness, but now she has to face herself! One of the most difficult aspects of the whole situation is that she finds herself being helplessly pulled along by the unfolding of this unexpected (and un-asked for) drama with no clear idea about how to proceed: just an endless stream of painful revelations and un-Christlike reactions that she never counted on having to face. It all seems so unfair! Surely this is not what God had in mind for marriage.

Although I realize it is a necessary part of the process the hurting wife must go through, the last thing I want to do is write about her failures. Of course she has failed in some areas; it would be crazy to think she wouldn't. But for heaven's sake! The poor woman is in the throes of a devastated marriage. She finds her life crumbling around her. Is it really necessary to get into all of this now? Well, the answer is "yes" because now is when this stuff is coming to the surface. Ever the merciful opportunist, the Lord wants to take full advantage of this situation to purge that poison out of her heart.

"But if it wasn't for my husband's failure, these attitudes wouldn't even be an issue! I am just responding to what has been thrust upon me." Well, in my humanistic heart I want to whole-heartedly agree, but in my spirit I would say, "The heart is deceitful above all things, and desperately wicked; who can know it?" (Jeremiah 17:9 NKJV) What is coming out of you isn't new, it's just been repackaged. Circumstances beyond your control have forced you to face what has been lying dormant in you all along. Contrary to what we want to believe about ourselves (and what the culture pushes on us), we are not inherently good. Like a tube of toothpaste, when pressure is applied, what is in us comes out—it can't help but do so.

I know it isn't fair; many things in this life aren't fair. The bottom line is if we are sincere in our hearts we will want Him to purge, purify and perfect us in and through our sufferings. Sincere believers see beyond the present and can discern a greater purpose in the trials of life.

The great thing about God is that He can bring about the absolute best out of any situation—nothing is wasted with Him. And by the way, if you don't like seeing your heart and if you find in yourself repulsion to this open-heart surgery form of purification, it's okay! His grace is sufficient for you, just like it is for your husband.

So, are you the appeasing wife, the enabling wife, the police wife or the angry wife? I was all four of them at one time or another. These categories are not absolute, but you will probably find that you will most closely identify either with the police/angry wife or the appeasing/enabling wife. And yet you might also find your emotions flip-flopping as you encounter different issues. One minute you might be full of anger and the next crying your eyes out. One day you will find yourself trying to control your husband's life and the next day you might feel very needy for his affection. It's just part of being a woman!

On that note, let's look at these four reactions.

THE POLICE WIFE

The police wife is a natural born "fixer." She is a problem solver and even if it isn't broken, a little tweak here and there never hurts! The black and white perspective she has in life is on high alert in a crisis such as this. She feels she has to stay on top of sudden changes and atmospheric conditions in her world and her children's world. She is a strong, no nonsense kind of woman and would bend over backwards for anyone that needs her help; but woe to him who tries to hurt her!

Phyllis tried to keep her husband on the straight-and-narrow but eventually realized it was affecting her more than his sin. "I would read his journal, his text messages, and his emails just to see if I could find something," she writes. "I was getting out of control. I didn't want to be his mother, but I had to know if he was struggling. I was trying to control his recovery."

Cassandra's story is a great illustration, not only of the fears that lie behind the need to control one's husband but also the insanity a police wife can get into. For instance, she would bend herself around the bannister at the top of the stairs to sneak a peek at what he was watching on TV—fully expecting to catch him gazing at some pretty girl and then she would "have him." When she would question what he was looking at, he would innocently say the news and the battle would begin. The interrogation about each "infomercial babe" would come at him in rapid fire. The hostility and anger from Cassandra caused instant friction and tension and, of course, the argument quickly ensued. There is no question that she was the cause of most of their arguments. As Cassandra tells it:

Jim and I had a very unique marriage from the very beginning. We did not have sex on our wedding night, nor on our honeymoon, nor for the first year and a half of our marriage. I just could not physically open up to my husband. My need for control and my lack of trust would not allow my body to do what it was meant to do. Also Satan is a liar and I was involved in one huge mind game. All of this caused resentment in my husband which played a part in his unfaithfulness.

Suspicions and fear ran my life from the first moment I found out Jim cheated on me. Every day I lived in fear that I would find something that would blow my world to pieces. Every call on his phone, every text, every second he was late, every time he wasn't home. I lived in fear that the women he'd been involved with—or even their boyfriends—were going to come to our home and hurt me. I was constantly waiting with bated breath for the floor of my heart to give way.

This fear drove me to become a detective. Now, if anything kept your heart racing and your blood pressure up it was the forever detective work of a scared wife. I checked his phone, constantly! I checked the home phone and Jim got an interrogation about the numbers on the caller ID. I went thru (sic) the phone bills with a fine-tooth comb and again interrogated him. I wanted to know where he was when he was five minutes late. I wanted to know why the bed covers were different when I got home from how I left them in the morning. I wanted to know why the computer was on when I left it off. Anything you can think of, I wanted and needed to know. It was draining and impossible to keep up with. And when it all fell apart, I felt like a failure. I was a terrible detective; I had not done my job.

The day that I let go of this was a very happy and freeing day. Thank you Jesus, no more worries! I have been a new woman ever since. I can't remember the last time I checked his phone for weird numbers. He is open and honest and I trust him. It may be the best feeling in the world!

I think all of us have a little police wife in us. Even as a classic enabler and appeaser, I still found myself searching for clues with Steve. There is an insane drive to find evidence. It's a mission to hunt down proof that what has been imagined is in fact going on. In a weird sort of way the police wife wants to have that "I knew it!" moment; and yet, at the same time, she desperately hopes it doesn't come. So much of this fact-finding mission is driven by fear and a desire to control one's circumstances.

Wives who are prone to deal with their situation by policing their husbands will need the Lord to adjust their perspectives. The fact of the matter is she cannot talk her husband into doing the right thing; she cannot shame him into being pure; and she cannot threaten him into honesty. What she must do is to learn to entrust him into the hands of the Lord. After all, only God can change his heart.

All of the ways she may try to help him: keeping him accountable for time, money, cell phone use and so on can be helpful in a mutually agreed upon situation. But she must be careful not to force her own regimen on him. It is effortless for the "police" wife to put herself into a role which only God can fill. It is also very common in such situations for her best efforts to backfire on her, provoking resentment in her husband and stripping him of the motivation to be honest with her. Instead of helping the situation, too much controlling only tends to create tension in the relationship. Not only does such badgering put the wife in the role of leader of the home, but it also tends to demoralize the husband in his own efforts to find lasting freedom.

It is so important that this woman learns to trust God in the situation. If she can harness all that zeal and turn it into prayer for her husband, the results can be astounding. His behavior will not change until his heart changes. Only the Holy Spirit can bring about that change. But, alas, it is so easy (for the flesh) to criticize and so hard to pray.

THE ANGRY WIFE

The emotion of anger manifests itself differently in people. Wives who have been hurt by the sin of their husbands tend to indulge this carnal passion in one of two ways. Strong-willed, forceful women tend to lash out in outbursts of rage. Wives who have more passive natures often "stuff" their feelings, allowing their anger to remain on "low boil."

It's not surprising that Cassandra—the ever-vigilant police wife—was also prone to explosions of anger. She shares what was going on with her:

Anger is an ugly, ugly monster just waiting to attack at the slightest hint of a problem. I brought my anger into our marriage. I screamed and yelled and said insanely hurtful things. It was an intense sin that I was letting control my very being. It all stems back to that one familiar word, control. By being angry all the time I could control the situation with Jim. I kept him in his place, kept him low, kept him guilty and punished for what he had done to me. I was relentless and horrible. Due to all those years of anger, all those years of letting my emotions fly when and where and how I wanted, I still struggle with outbursts. I still have to consciously, every day, stop myself from yelling. It is a habit that I pray will be broken soon.

Lois's struggles were more low-key but just as serious. "I still struggle with anger and bitterness every time I pass by a motel or place where I know or even suspect he's been with someone else," she says. "It's hard to let it go, but I'm recognizing more often that it's my sin that wants to hold onto the anger and bitterness. I want him to pay me back for all the harm I think he's caused me. I want to be on the pedestal and have him worship me and grovel at my feet."

However the anger manifests itself, unforgiveness lies at the root of it. The wife has been deeply hurt, even devastated by her husband's actions. She has been hurt in what is likely the most sensitive area of a woman's soul: her husband's devotion and faithfulness. When someone has been hurt like this, it is only natural to build walls around one's heart. However, Christians are still expected to obey God.

It takes little effort to cave in to feelings of bitterness. It is so easy to hate when you've been hurt or violated in some way, but Jesus teaches us a better way to respond to such mistreatment: He said, "For if you forgive men for their transgressions, your heavenly Father will also forgive you. But if you do not forgive men, then your Father will not forgive your transgressions." (Matthew 6:14-15) This is where it must begin: forgiveness. In order to be right with God herself, the wife must be willing to forgive her husband regardless of the sins he has committed.

Throughout His earthly ministry, Jesus dealt less with outward behavior and more with people's hearts. With precision, He went right to the root issue buried deep within a person's inner life. Like a two-edged sword, His words pierced through dividing the soul and spirit, judging the thoughts and intents of the heart. In Matthew 5, when He talked about heart adultery, He was showing lust-filled men the depravity of their hearts. It was the same thing with anger. He said that if you are angry at someone, you are in the exact same spirit as a murderer. The words of Jesus expose our hearts and reveal what hypocrites we can be. We judge according to outward appearances, but God looks upon the heart.

Forgiveness is the same. I realize the wife is struggling with feelings of betrayal and bitterness. Who wouldn't, considering what she has had to endure? But feelings come and go; the Lord is more concerned with what is occurring in the heart. Forgiveness is a process that takes time. I don't mean to imply that we are excused for ever being unforgiving. What I mean is that it takes time for the wife to feel like she can trust her husband again. Because he is the one who broke that trust, the burden is on his shoulders to re-establish a relationship built upon trust and truthfulness.

The forgiving wife wants her husband to make it, does everything she can to encourage him and therefore expects him to take the situation seriously. A wife who is unforgiving, on the other hand, continually reminds him of his past offenses and anticipates his constant failure. This of course, only serves to further demoralize him and retard his efforts to get free. The idol in the heart of an unforgiving wife is s-e-l-f. She is far more concerned about protecting herself from ever being hurt again, than she is about restoring her marriage or supporting her husband in his struggle to overcome sexual sin. Even if your husband continues to struggle and fail, that does not mean you have earned the right to be unforgiving and angry; your heart is still an issue. Yes, it is very painful to watch him fail, but, for your own sake, you must gain a biblical perspective on the situation.

Any woman unwilling to forgive is closing herself off from the God of love. The need to repay the husband for the suffering he has caused will only keep the wife in a prison every bit as evil as the bondage to sexual sin her husband has been in.

THE APPEASING WIFE

If the police wife is on high alert at all times and ready to face down any obstacle that comes her way, the appeasing wife would be considered the exact opposite. Rather than being the detective who is bent on finding out the complete truth, she tends to avoid painful facts. By nature, she is a "peace at any cost" person. For myself, as an appeasing wife, I believed all my efforts to "keep the peace" and deliver a non-ballistic approach would surely win the day. The appeasing wife doesn't want to know what is really happening. It is unbearable to face the fact that her husband is interested in others and that her marriage is crumbling. She would prefer to throw all such bad news into a file buried somewhere in the back of her mind. She has an amazing ability to reduce the enormous elephant in her living room down to the size of a mouse.

Not only does she inwardly minimize the seriousness of the situation, but she does this in the way she interacts with her husband. She will do her utmost to relieve tension in the relationship. If it means she must overlook obvious sin, placate a bothered conscience or humor him in his depression, she will do so if it means keeping the peace. In fact, she would rather endure his emotional bullying than to try to take a stand for what is right.

An appeasing wife is so emotionally dependent upon her husband that she cannot imagine life without him and will do almost anything to keep him. Her value and worth come from keeping him happy and having his approval. Rather than receiving her value and worth as a person from the Lord, she looks for it from her husband. Thus, if he is happy with her, she feels good about herself. If he is dissatisfied with her, she feels badly about herself.

When a wife like this discovers that her husband has an obsession with other women, she is devastated and often blames herself for his self-centered behavior. She does not understand that his behavior has nothing whatsoever to do with her. His problem would rear its ugly head even if he was married to the most gorgeous woman in the world. Of course, a sexual addict married to a woman who aims to appease will often capitalize on this emotional weakness for his own self-serving purposes.

As she frantically scrambles to save her marriage, she will often enter into his secret life with him. This wife may start viewing pornography with her husband, thinking this will help keep him satisfied at home. She hasn't a clue as to how much of a catalyst pornography is—that it fans the flames of lust already at work inside him. Of course, once she allows him to take her through that door there will be no stopping him.

Phyllis did this. "I thought I would 'spice things' up and brought *The Joy of Sex* into our bedroom and would occasionally watch some porn with him. I now know this was a horrible mistake that opened us both up to the enemy. It didn't help anything."

Again, the appeasing wife will do anything she can to keep her husband. With a misguided sense of duty as a wife, she will try her utmost to accommodate her husband's demanding nature—even though she continues to get terribly hurt in the process.

While it may seem as though she is simply being forgiving and Christlike, the real truth is that she is only really concerned about protecting herself. Since peace is what she wants, she will not take a stand or demand any change from her husband. Ultimately, she is not nearly as concerned with his spiritual welfare as she is about her own feelings. She might continue to be warm and friendly, but she will not allow the relationship to go beyond a superficial level. She is determined not to make herself vulnerable to her husband. The reality is that she is emotionally detaching herself from him. The problem with that is that if her heart is closed to him, it is also closed to the Lord. She is depending on her "peaceful" nature and nice personality rather than depending on the Lord to help her and heal her. Sadly, she mistakes her "niceness" for God-likeness.

Hopefully, at some point she will develop enough godly love and concern for her husband that she will confront him in his sin. This, of course, is the last thing she wants to do. Confrontation is extremely difficult for this woman for two reasons. First, she is generally weak in that area of her life, anyway. She goes through life trying to avoid discord with *anybody*. The thought of standing up to a domineering husband is very intimidating. The other reason that confronting her husband's sin would be difficult is her fear that he would walk out on her. She is so emotionally dependent on him she would be at a total loss if she had to live without him.

For me, I needed to get to the place in my heart that I would rather be single for the rest of my life than to continue in the sinful lifestyle we were maintaining. It was then that I began to do what was best for Steve. That is when I walked out on him! I took a stand and refused to let him control and dominate me. I was no longer willing to cover up for him and act like everything was okay. Everything wasn't okay; it was terribly broken and that is not the life I wanted. I didn't quite grasp how much trouble he was in spiritually, but I knew he was a mess and I wasn't helping him by just "going along" with his sinful lifestyle. Taking that stand was exactly what we both needed.

THE ENABLER WIFE

This wife's issues are so closely related to those of the appeasing wife it is difficult to differentiate between the two. Perhaps these are simply two different attributes to the same person.

Synonyms of the word enabler provide a good foundation to begin this section: qualify, endue, equip, strengthen, authorize, warrant, accredit, validate, sanction, approve, give the go ahead. All of these terms describe how this wife handles her husband's indiscretions. I, myself, have to lower my head and raise my hand: guilty again! I didn't make a career out of it, but at one point I made it easy for my husband to have his cake and eat it too!

Trying to keep the peace at any cost is the underlying motive for both the appeaser's and the enabler's actions. It's a great quality when the Spirit is leading, but when it is just a personality trait fueled by fear and weakness it becomes corrupt.

The enabler's method of pain management is ignorance. She would rather overlook the facts staring her in the face than deal with them. "Bill would make promises about many things with absolutely no intention of keeping them," recalls Lois. "I always believed him because I loved him and wanted to believe him."

The emphasis here is "I wanted to believe him." At face value that is a Christ-like characteristic, but actually this statement simply reflects more head-in-the-sand thinking. It's just a "gloss job" for not wanting to dig too deeply or demand too much.

The Enabler Wife simply doesn't want to acknowledge the glaring red flags she is seeing. The thought of infidelity is so painful and overwhelming that she simply shuts it out of her mind. It is easier for her to stifle her suspicions than to have to deal with them head-on.

Let's face it, when a woman discovers that her husband has been chronically unfaithful there are no easy solutions. For one thing she is devastated. So, of course, pretending that there is no adultery helps to escape that pain. Deep down inside, the hurting wife knows that she will have to make some very painful decisions. But many women are simply too dependent upon their husbands to even consider leaving them. Others are too weak to confront their husbands. The easiest recourse is to simply act as though there isn't a problem and hope that it will resolve itself.

The unfortunate consequence to this kind of reaction is that nothing ever happens to force the husband to deal with his sin. His wife's lack of response allows him to keep his home *and* his mistresses: every adulterer's dream. Since his wife won't confront him and doesn't force him to decide between her and his sin, he is able to keep them both.

But there is an issue that is even greater than the pain: her husband is very likely lost and on his way to hell. That could be a high price to pay so that she can shrink to the path of least resistance. It also exposes the selfishness in the Enabler Wife's heart to leave him in such a predicament, for the sake of maintaining her image and comfort zone.

"I got suspicious when screens that Jed was viewing on the computer would suddenly disappear when I walked into the room," recounts Sue. "It was humiliating. Sometimes I would let him know my suspicions. Other times I just pretended I hadn't even noticed. My unwillingness to confront him gave him free reign to do what he wanted without question. He easily hid it from me because I closed my eyes to the truth. His problem was not my fault but it was important that I take an active stance in our healing."

So, what's a girl to do who doesn't want to do anything? DO SOMETHING! Part of the *modus operandi* for these women is to avoid every thought about the situation because it is too painful. This denial is even taken to the point of not praying about it—the very thing that is most needed! But this is the very thing she must do: pray, pray, pray. And when she has finished praying, she must pray some more! She must pray earnestly, fervently and with passion that God will give her eyes to see, ears to hear and the heart to step up to the plate and do what she can to help rescue this perishing soul. Something more important than her feelings and comfort zone has to take front seat. She must find the courage to get outside of herself and allow God to transform her weak inability into a loving, concerned, willingness to deal with the issue.

All this boils down to a lack of godly love. This woman might convince herself that her way of expressing love is to be accepting, but the truth is that this attitude is the very opposite of true love. When you love someone, you do what's best for their wellbeing. A woman who has the natural tendency to appease must be very honest with herself about the motivations of her actions.

If she will be honest, she will acknowledge that she is more concerned about gaining her husband's affections than she is about obeying God. This kind of dependent relationship is simply another form of idolatry.

So there you have it: four different natural reactions to a husband involved in sexual sin. There is a common denominator in all of these responses: they are all "natural." In other words, they are the way a woman's fallen nature would deal with her particular situation. The key then is for the hurting wife to force herself out of her own comfort zone and find the "God zone." His way of facing this kind of situation will not only be the best for the husband, but it will also be the best for the wife as well.

7

THE PLACE OF
GOD'S WORD

*"O Lord, help me to look to Your Word
alone for my answers."*

Crisis has a way of provoking panic in a person. If you are a wife who has just discovered that your husband has been involved in sexual sin, chances are you are, at least to some degree, in crisis mode. Or perhaps you've been dealing with this for a long time and you are just tired, worn out and fatigued by the whole mess. In either case, the typical reaction is to go into damage control.

A wife in the midst of such a crisis is understandably desperate to find answers. But in her frantic condition she tends to grab anything that comes along. She listens intently to sermons; she reads books about marriage or sexual sin; she will even invite the counsel of those who have no wisdom or experience in such matters. She will get online and spend hours searching for help for her husband, help for herself and help for her kids. Her heart and ears are bent toward anything that could be the "silver bullet" that will cause the pain to go away and offer the perfect solution to her dilemma.

It is invaluable in such a season to remember that God uses crises to test a person's heart and life. In other words, the emergencies we face as believers serve as a barometer of where we are spiritually. How a person reacts in these situations shows the level of her spiritual health.

A healthy Christian will experience the pain and the fear that the crisis introduces, but she will not be dominated by these feelings. If she has a solid walk with God, she discovers she has an inner strength that helps her to cope maturely. She may experience setbacks and struggles, but if she is centered in the Lord she will always find her way back to the Source of life and wisdom.

In the midst of crisis, she will be able to make wise decisions: decisions she will not regret later; decisions that will lead her closer to God. Of course, scripturally speaking, the alternative to wisdom is foolishness. Now before you get mad and throw the book across the room, please hear me out! Let me explain what this Hebraic term means and why we as hurting wives need to give it due consideration.* There are two characteristics that emerge in a biblical study of the word "fool."

First, the term has the connotation of being "open." In other words, this person is open to whatever comes along. And when you think about it, isn't this one of the main reasons we have lost respect for our husbands—that rather than being guarded and exclusive with their affections, they left a spot in their hearts open to additional possibilities? In our case, we need to ask ourselves if we have left a spot in our hearts open to counsel that will lead us away from doing what is pleasing to God. Are we unguarded in what or who we allow to influence us?

The other common characteristic of a foolish person is one who lives for the moment. Here again we can easily point at our husbands and yell, "Guilty! This fool lived his life for momentary pleasure—no matter what it would cost him in the long run!" Yet, we too must be careful that we don't look for

* There are actually a number of Hebrew words translated as "fool" in our Old Testament. They all point to essentially the same thing: one who is unwise.

solutions to our problems that appeal to our emotions while offering only short-term relief. In other words, we need answers that are firmly based in Scripture.

"Listen, I believe in the Bible, but what does that have to do with the dilemma I am currently facing in my marriage?" you might ask. Well, the role you allow Scripture to have in this situation is actually of extreme importance. With that in mind, I want to address two different areas where the Word of God needs to play an enormous part in this crisis: your personal, spiritual wellbeing and where you turn for answers.

THE STAPLE OF LIFE

King David made a comment once that is so true! He wrote, "The law of the Lord is perfect, restoring the soul; the testimony of the Lord is sure, making wise the simple." (Psalm 19:7) First and foremost, we have to decide if we really believe that statement. I for one want to say that I unequivocally attest to the truth it expresses!

Our souls have been shattered by the devastating effects of our husbands' infidelity. We don't need emotional band aids; we need deep restoration.

Many professing Christians, however, don't really have a solid, ongoing relationship with Scripture. So when faced with crisis—if they look to their Bible at all—it is to sort of superstitiously open it up and plop their finger down on a random page in the hopes that God will speak to them. Or they may rummage through it like a child running through a toy store—superficially glancing at everything on the shelves but not really looking intently at any one thing.

I want to offer you a completely different approach. I want to encourage you to use the Bible to regain (or deepen) your spiritual and emotional health. Earlier I said, "A healthy Christian will experience the pain and the fear that the crisis introduces, but she will not be dominated by these feelings." The Word of God is the key to subduing her myriad and sometimes conflicting emotions. This is the kind of spiritual health which will help a hurting wife weather such a storm.

As you make the Word of God a vital part of your daily life, it will begin to build a spiritual structure within you. It will deepen God's righteous standard and perspective. It will shape your thinking and affect your decisions. But I must tell you, for it to have this kind of effect in your life you must spend meaningful time in the Word every day. If your time in Scripture is nothing more than sporadically reading a little bit of it here and there, even when you do encounter a spiritual truth relevant to your situation it will have no meaningful impact on you. It will seem like just another opinion you have accumulated along the way.

What you need right now is to ingest a daily meal of trustworthy truth that the Holy Spirit can use to strengthen you spiritually. This will, in turn, strengthen you emotionally. God's Word should not be seen as a quick fix for this crisis. Rather, it should be part of developing a spiritually healthy lifestyle. Remember, it is the "law of the Lord" (a biblical synonym for Scripture) that restores the soul.

There is nothing written that is more powerful, authoritative or reliable than the Word of God. You could search your whole life and never find anything else that will answer the longing in your heart because it alone is where you find the Lord and where you come to intimately know Him.

According to the first chapter of John's gospel, the Word of God actually is Jesus Christ. In other words, the Bible we hold in our hands and read and refer to and study is revealing Jesus Christ to us—God incarnate. He is the Word—it is He whom the Scriptures are talking about. If we have a weak relationship with Scripture it's probably because we have a weak relationship with the Lord. But the opposite is true as well: if we have a meaningful walk with Christ it's because we have found Him in His Word. I can't properly express just how amazing it is that we have this treasure in our hands!

THE AUTHORITY OF GOD'S WORD

In my husband's book *A Biblical Guide to Counseling the Sexual Addict*, he recounts the story of the November 2000 elections and the debacle of that election. The title of that chapter is "The Method of Our Counsel," and it makes the important point of how critical it is for the Word of God to be the basis of our decision-making in life and in counseling:

Who could ever forget November 11, 2000, when the entire presidential election came down to the state of Florida? George W. Bush was eventually declared the winner of that state—and of the presidential race. However, Al Gore's attorneys appealed to the liberal Florida Supreme Court, coaxing them to write new laws in their favor that would give them the election. In the meantime, Democratic "spin-doctors" made the rounds on television talk shows attempting to incite a public outcry over the "terrible injustice" that had occurred. They created such a cloud of confusion that the average American completely lost sight of the fact that there are existing laws in place to deal with such matters.

Eventually, the United States Supreme Court stepped into the brouhaha and in essence said, "Wait a minute. You cannot just make new laws for the sake of convenience. It does not matter what is the current public opinion. Polls have no relevance in such matters. Dan Rather's opinion does not make a difference. The only determining factor in this is what is written in the Constitution." Thank God we have an immovable legal charter that establishes rock-solid guidelines about how to run our nation! If it weren't for the Constitution, every decision lawmakers faced would be continually subject to the whims of the current pop culture.

In the same way, when it comes to determining the best course of action for a believer struggling with sin, it is imperative that the counselor uses the Word of God—not simply as the ultimate authority on such matters—but also as an actual handbook of solutions.[1]

This is a good piece of advice for wives in crisis. Without God's Word, we will face the situation in a state of complete confusion. One person's word is as good as another's if we do not give Scripture its proper place in our thinking.

A hurting wife is in an extremely vulnerable period of her life. All that remains of her marriage is a terrible pile of rubble. When her world has been blasted to pieces she is not necessarily going to be thinking rationally. In that despairing condition she is desperate for answers. "God, please show me what to do!" she cries. "Give me relief, and I don't care where it comes from!"

Therein lays the danger. Unless you have learned to run to the Word of God with every problem, you will probably run to everything else first and the Bible only as a last resort. Even many who have been Christians for years turn to "empty cisterns" (Jeremiah 2:13) in an attempt to pull their lives back together.

We women are especially prone to turn to teachers who can touch us emotionally. Unfortunately, this tendency can lead us to make disastrous mistakes. If we allow our feelings to guide us and seek out those who merely soothe our emotions, we will surely end up in a ditch.

The great need for wives who have been devastated is a source of trustworthy wisdom. Therefore, we must be very careful that whatever advice we are receiving—whether it comes in the form of a book or through a counselor—be entirely based on Scripture. Considering the gravity of the situation, we cannot afford to be casual about where we turn for answers.

This means we must come to grips with what we really believe. The Bible is not neutral about its approach to life and neither should we be neutral in our approach to it. The most effective form of deception is the mixture of truth and error. This is an ageless ploy of the enemy. The devil will take a grain of truth—just enough to give his words a degree of legitimacy—and then will add in his deception.

Herein lies one of the great challenges we face today: finding teachers who have the mature discernment which only comes through spending long hours in Scripture. There is a vast difference between someone who has learned how to use the Bible as a teaching tool and someone who lives his or her daily life in subjection to it. A godly person speaks out of what God has put into their heart. As Jesus said, "The good man brings out of his good treasure what is good; and the evil man brings out of his evil treasure what is evil." (Matthew 12:35)

One of the things that has most grieved my husband and I over our past three decades of ministry is the number of teachers operating within the Body of Christ who actually treat the Bible with a certain degree of disdain. Oh, you will never hear them say anything blatantly disrespectful about it; they simply don't allow it to have its proper place in their personal lives or in their ministries. Their wisdom operates in the soulish realm of emotions and feelings. God's Word, on the other hand, is a spiritual tool which operates within a person's heart, spirit and will.

The truth of the matter is that anyone who treats man's opinions (i.e. the teachings of psychotherapy, etc.) on the same level as the holy Bible is arrogant and lacks faith. A person who lives his life with faith in Christ gives the Word of God its proper authority in his or her life. Here is where faith triumphs—where mere human reasoning stumbles—holding fast the Word of Truth. If you believe, as so many do, that the Word of God is just not enough, you are already doomed to go the way of the world; that of leaning on the broken-reed-teachings of man.

So what do you do? If you see that you have disregarded and counted His Word a common thing, just another addition to your cache of other "helpful" information, I urge you to simply repent. You can turn away from the broken cisterns of this world and set yourself on a course of trusting in the Lord and His Word.

Your faith in the authority of Scripture must be supreme in the entirety of your life. Time spent in the Bible builds the kind of faith you desperately need right now. There is something supernatural about a humble heart approaching God's Word with the expectation that He wants to impart something to you. Those who come to the Word as just another resource have done themselves harm and will receive little if anything from it. The Word of God is living and active—it is unlike anything else.

So as you work your way through the tremendous challenges you will face in the days ahead, I want to encourage you to go to the greatest source of wisdom you will ever find: the Word of the living God!

CHOOSING FAITH OVER FEAR

"O Lord, help me choose to act in faith and not in fear."

Let's set aside the impact of your husband's sexual sin for just a moment and talk about one of the most powerful emotions a person can experience: fear. One could compare fear to anger, or even lust, in the sense that, if it is allowed to go unrestrained, it has the ability to completely take control of a person's thinking. Gender has nothing to do with it—both men and women are highly susceptible to being dominated by fear. Being married to a husband involved in sexual sin only exacerbates the problem of fear that every wife already contends with.

It probably goes without saying that God instilled the capacity for fear within our makeup as a way to alert us to danger. Biologically speaking, when a person senses some form of peril, their adrenal glands secrete adrenaline into the bloodstream causing their heartrate and blood pressure to increase, which, in turn, sends a surge of blood to the muscles. This surge can account for stories you've probably heard of people exerting what seems to be superhuman strength or amazing agility in the face of life or death situations. It is all part of the remarkable system God created within the human body.

However, fear can operate in a less intense manner as well. Take worry, for example. Worry is a low-level form of fear that occurs when a person feels anxious about concerns or problems, whether they are real or only perceived. It creates a nagging, incessant, unconscious feeling that people usually acquiesce to and learn to live with.

I mention worry because this type of fear is common with wives, especially when it comes to what goes on in their home. After all, we have been wired to be concerned about marriage and family. Our lives revolve around our families, and anything that threatens those relationships can quickly become a source of significant apprehension. That natural fretting can easily overtake a person's faith and lead to despair and even debilitating anxiety.

Most chronic worriers don't look for help from the Lord about their fears because they've become accustomed to them. They have always dealt with their problems through worry. Let's face it: *it takes less effort to sit and fret than to kneel and pray.* When women are imprisoned by fear, it is because they are relying on their own abilities (which are obviously inadequate) to handle their problems instead of turning their cares over to the One who really can help them. When we wives allow our problems to dominate our thinking, God seems very small and powerless to us. We effectively make our problems and fears bigger than God.

It may be painful to admit it, but when you get right down to it, the root of fear really is self-preservation and self-centeredness—being preoccupied with our own life. It is not uncommon for a wife to be far more concerned about how her husband's sinful behavior is affecting her than how it might doom him eternally.

The truth of the matter is that fear rarely produces anything of value in a Christian. It excludes God from the picture and makes a wife rely on her own thinking to come up with a solution to her problems. It keeps her stuck in herself and distant from the Lord. The apostle John said, "There is no fear in love; but perfect love casts out fear, because fear involves punishment, and the one who fears is not perfected in love." (1 John 4:18) Allowing it to dominate your mind not only will bring you into emotional torment, but it will also strip you of your ability to selflessly love those around you. If your focus in life is all about protecting yourself, you will not allow God's love to flow through you to your husband—the very thing he desperately needs that will encourage him to change!

One of the worst aspects of anxiety is that it can, over time, transform the person's character. In this respect, it operates in much the same way that lust does in a man's life. As it is given free rein to operate within a woman, it grows in strength and intensity. As it becomes stronger within the hurting wife, it can show up in different ways in her life. It can drive some women into anger and bitterness. Anxiousness can move some wives into a "peace at any cost" attitude with their husbands. Other women withdraw emotionally from loved ones—especially the husband who is creating the problems. Still others turn to drugs, drinking or even adultery as a way of dealing with it. Years of suppressed fear can even cause some women to develop health problems. Whatever else it might bring, it will certainly make her increasingly more self-focused.

I'VE BEEN THERE!

I know what it's like to be paralyzed and controlled by fear; for several years it held me in its icy grip. At the time, I did not realize how much it was living out its tyrannical life within me. It just became part of my life with Steve. It became like a mountain, its shadow affecting every other area of my life.

Those were difficult days. I simply did not have the emotional or spiritual maturity to deal with all of the stuff that was coming at me. First there were the mysterious telltale signs that something wasn't right in our marriage. Much of this confusion went away when Steve confessed the secret life of sexual sin he had been maintaining. Then, as he went back to hiding his behavior, I kept making new discoveries—each of which were stinging jabs at my heart, new sources of devastation. Throughout this entire ordeal I simply processed information as it came to me—never taking the time to think through (let alone pray through) a strategy as to how to best deal with all of this.

Rather than going to the Lord to find out how I should handle the situation, I simply allowed my fear of losing Steve to consume me. It never occurred to me at the time that I should be resisting and pushing back on it. I just allowed it to dominate my thinking. At the time I didn't realize it was a sin to worry.

When I did begin praying about our marriage, my supplications usually took the form of "worry prayers." I would ask the Lord to change him, but if I'm honest about it, I only prayed in the hopes that this source of pain to myself would go away.

I was an emotional wreck, praying mostly out of panic and fear. Rather than allowing the situation to drive me to dependence on the Lord, I allowed it to control my life. I became the center in many ways—and I was not really thinking about what was happening to Steve. I wasn't as concerned for his soul as I was about how his behavior was affecting me.

I was so consumed by my failing marriage that I had completely lost sight of the fact that I was going downhill spiritually at a very rapid rate.

It never occurred to me that I should be asking the Lord to set me free of the grip of fear on my heart. It took me a long time to even see the need to deal with it. I had become so accustomed to the constant anxiety that I was convinced I had a right to it. I saw myself as being the helpless victim of an overwhelming feeling I could not control because I could not make my husband change the behavior that was causing it.

The worst part of all of it was that I had made an idol out of my husband and my marriage. Instead of allowing God to take the central position in my life, I had given that place to Steve. What he thought of me not only was the most important thing in my life, but it was what gave the fear its strength in my heart. Because he was so obsessed with other women, I lived with the constant fear that he would find another woman he wanted more than me. I had allowed my marriage to become more sacred than my relationship to Jesus. I was in real trouble.

I eventually got to the place where, in sheer desperation, I began turning to the Lord in a very real way. I realized that I could not control or change my husband and walk with the Lord at the same time: I had to choose between the two. It was then that the Lord began to show me that my fear was based in a lack of trust in Him; therefore, it was sinful. Believe it or not, that was wonderful news because I came to realize that I was no longer a helpless victim with no hope of ever overcoming my fears. If it was a sin then it meant I had a way out. I could repent of it and ask the Lord to help me overcome it. With repentance as a starting point, the Lord was now able to become much more involved in the situation.

I confessed that I had not been trusting the Lord but had been trusting in myself. I asked the Lord to forgive me for this and resolved to change the way I lived my life. Once I experienced this repentance, the way I dealt with Steve completely changed. I quit watching, waiting and fretting. To a large degree I started overlooking obvious stuff that previously would have crushed me—those things that had tied me in knots inside. I had to make a very conscious decision to quit reacting to Steve and turn my heart and mind to the Lord. It was hard at times. I didn't just sail through it, but I was also no longer a slave to fear either. My walk with the Lord grew; my faith grew; I was now standing on solid ground.

TURNING IT AROUND

One of the things that really woke me up was when I realized that I was more afraid of losing Steve than missing God. In other words, Steve was the one I absolutely *had* to have, even if it meant forfeiting God's presence in my life. This revelation terrified me and really helped turn around my thinking. It can do the same for you as well.

How are we affected when we miss God? We shrivel up spiritually. We become so distracted and paralyzed that we can hardly function in life. We start falling apart emotionally. Our prayer life is minimal, weak or non-existent. If we even spend time in the Word it seems dry and lifeless. Moods, feelings and tempers rule our lives. In other words, we are living in the flesh. We are becoming increasingly more earthly-minded. The atmosphere in the home is heavy. Tempers flare up. When we know things aren't right, we take that as our cue to investigate, to monitor and to see what's up. What we don't realize is this course of action is taking us somewhere—away from the Presence of the Lord. There is no faith when panic and fear are in control.

So you can see why fearful living is sinful living. It is the opposite of trusting the Lord. How is it possible to obey the commandment to, "Trust in the Lord with all your heart, and do not lean on your own understanding. In all your ways acknowledge Him…" (Proverbs 3:5-6a) when you are consumed with your husband's behavior? You cannot live your life trying to control your husband and trust the Lord at the same time; it's not possible.

The fact of the matter is that the Bible commands believers not to fear. In his book, *Facing the Future without Fear*, Lloyd Ogilvie claims there are 366 "fear nots" in the Bible—one "fear not" for every day of the year.[1] Actually, if you did a word search on "do not fear" or "do not be afraid," you would only find a little over 100 references to those specific phrases. However, the concept of not allowing fear to control you really is found throughout Scripture.

One of the strongest passages that deals with the subject is found in the book of Luke:

> I say to you, My friends, do not be afraid of those who kill the body and after that have no more that they can do. But I will warn you whom to fear: fear the One who, after He has killed, has authority to cast into hell; yes, I tell you, fear Him! Are not five sparrows sold for two cents? Yet not one of them is forgotten before God. Indeed, the very hairs of your head are all numbered. Do not fear; you are more valuable than many sparrows. (Luke 12:4-7)

Okay, there it is: "Do not be afraid" and "do not fear." These are commandments and if we disregard them and allow fear to dominate our hearts and minds, then we are sinning. But if it is sin we have hope because there is something we can do: we can repent. The word "repent" in the New Testament literally means "to think again, to change one's thinking." And that perfectly describes what is called for in this type of situation: a whole new mindset!

This is where a solid devotional life is so greatly needed. You will never be able to properly handle such an overwhelming problem unless you are walking in the Spirit. It is so important to be solidly attached to the Vine. You need a steady diet of the Word of God to help you to think biblically, to strengthen yourself spiritually and emotionally. You need prayer to stay plugged into God's daily supply of grace and mercy. It takes ongoing communion with Him to gain His perspective for yourself, for your marriage and for your husband. It is at the feet of Jesus that you will adopt His mindset. Faith in Him will overcome the fear of being hurt by your husband. Jesus is not an add-on! He has to be given the central place in your heart and you have to give it to Him.

The Old Testament word for repentance literally means "to turn." It is usually used with the idea of turning away from sin or idolatry and turning to the Lord. If your situation is anything like mine was, you need to repent of not trusting in the Lord as well as the idolatry you have made of your marriage.

But it also means "to turn" in a very real way: to turn away from the idol of marriage and turn toward the Lord. This may require you at some level to take your hands off the control panel, to let go of the monitoring system. This is more than just throwing up your hands in defeat—it should be a declaration of faith: "I will put my trust in You, Lord, no matter what comes my way."

Let's face it; it doesn't take any effort to be in fear. It comes very naturally when we're in a potentially painful situation. To fear takes no more effort than it takes to get angry or, for that matter, for your husband to give in to lustful thoughts. Going against those natural feelings is not going to be effortless. It will require determination and commitment.

Faith, on the other hand, is not natural. It is supernatural. Having faith in the Lord for salvation does not come naturally; in fact everything about the Christian life is supernatural. And it is supernatural living that you need to be able to battle through this ordeal in the right way. To mature spiritually and to walk with the Lord you must cultivate your faith—it doesn't just happen. You must pursue the Lord and make a determined effort to give him the central place in your heart.

"You will keep him in perfect peace," Isaiah explained, "Whose mind is stayed on You, because he trusts in You." (Isaiah 26:3 NKJV) That really does describe perfectly what is called for here: to fix our hearts and minds on the Lord and to trust Him with our lives.

If you will begin making a concerted effort to walk with God and put your faith in Him, you will find your entire outlook changing. The dark clouds of fear and doubt will begin to dissipate. Hope for the future will start to rise within your heart. You will be in a position spiritually to fight for your marriage in believing prayer. You will find yourself living above the circumstances of your life. In fact, you will find that you no longer feel enslaved to your husband's behavior.

Repent of being fixated on your husband's sin. Turn to the Lord and you will find an atmosphere of faith filling your heart.

9

THE NOBILITY OF A
WOMAN

*"O Lord, replace all petty selfishness
within me with godly character."*

God has a great call on your life. No, I'm not referring to you becoming involved in formal ministry. What I'm talking about is a special invitation to become all that He has envisioned you to be as a woman. While it is certainly a lofty goal, it is also very attainable.

If you are to fulfill this great call, you will be required to make a deliberate choice. It will not occur by happenstance. In fact, the natural default built into your fallen nature—and enthusiastically supported by our fallen culture—is in direct contradiction to God's purposes. You will never be the woman He has in mind for you to be simply by going with the flow of American life. You will have to make a conscious decision to go a different path.

The beginning of this new direction comes about through understanding the way that comes naturally—the way of the world, the flesh and the devil. Let's begin by looking at a few quotes that seem to sum up the world's trendy notion of womanhood:

> "One of the things about equality is not just that you
> be treated equally to a man, but that you treat yourself
> equally to the way you treat a man."
>
> **—Marlo Thomas**[1]

"Women are the only exploited group in history to have been idealized into powerlessness."

—*Erica Jong*[2]

"Any intelligent woman who reads the marriage contract, and then goes into it, deserves all the consequences."

—*Isadora Duncan*[3]

"Marriage is for women the commonest mode of livelihood, and the total amount of undesired sex endured by women is probably greater in marriage than in prostitution."

—*Bertrand Russell, Marriage and Morals*[4]

"One does not have to sleep with, or even touch, someone who has paid for your meal. All those obligations are hereby rendered null and void."

—*Cynthia Heimel, Sex Tips for Girls*[5]

I think you get the general drift of what our society has adopted as its perspective of a woman's role in life. The common viewpoint of the marital relationship is the cohabitation of two people who share identical roles, have equal say in all decisions and hold their own personal desires as superior to the marriage itself.

In our day the noteworthy woman is independent and not afraid or ashamed to look out for herself. She is not chained to the old ways of being dependent on a man for security, love and protection. She has been so liberated from the traditional role of a woman that she deems it to be repugnant.

In his exposition of Proverbs 31 as presented in a sermon (from 1988) entitled "An Excellent Wife," John MacArthur well summarizes the difference between the biblical concept of womanhood and that of our modern culture. Some of it is offered in hyperbolic style but I think you will get the drift:

What kind of a woman does our society honor? Who is the honored woman of the eighties? Who is the prototype woman of the eighties? What is the modern super-woman like? If our society and our culture could design a woman, what would that woman be like?

Well let me see if I can't pull it together for you. She would work at a job, build her own career, demand and get equal pay with men. She would refuse to submit to her husband, demanding equality with him in everything. She would have an affair or two or three, a divorce or two or three, an abortion or two. She would definitely exercise her independence. She would make sure that she was imminently fulfilled herself. She would rely on her own resources. She would not want her husband or children to threaten her personal goals. She would have her own bank account. She would hire a maid or cleaning service. She would eat out at least 50 percent of the time with her family or without… She would be shopping to keep up with the fashion trends and make sure she could compete in the attention getting contest. She would put her children in a day-care center, making sure that each one also had a TV in his or her room so that when they were home they wouldn't interrupt her routine. She would be opinionated. She would demand to be heard from and eager to fulfill all of her personal ambition. The world would applaud her and she wouldn't be able to stay married or happy and her kids would probably be into drugs. But she would be the woman of the eighties. And she is a million miles from the woman of God described in Proverbs 31.

The woman described here is of priceless value. She

has physical strength, mental strength, moral strength and spiritual strength. Above all she loves God deeply and reverently....This is the woman that every woman should seek to emulate. She is rare, look at verse 10, an excellent wife....By the way, the word excellent in Hebrew means force, a woman of force, a woman of substance, a woman of strength would be another way to characterize her. It's excellent in the sense of her strength spiritually, morally, mentally, physically. She is a woman of substance. She is a woman who has made a dent in society. She is one who makes a difference. There's a force about her life. This kind of wife, he says, who can find? Very rare. Hard to find this kind of woman....

She loves the family and she loves her husband and it's the love of her heart that puts delight in her work. If she felt like the reason for her to live was to fulfill herself, everything she had to do for someone else she'd hate. But because she knows her reason to be is to give herself for the joy of those she loves, the delight of her heart becomes the delight of her hands.[6]

I think you can see the contrast. We have to decide which path we are going to take in life. Will we follow along the world's "me first" mentality or will we live the life that God has ordained for us? If we are going to be followers of Christ, we must follow in His ways. A. W. Pink, who lived a century ago, succinctly summed up these two directions in life:

The way of the world is self seeking and self-shielding. "Spare thyself" is the sum of its philosophy. But the doctrine of Christ is not "save thyself" but sacrifice thyself. There is no such thing as belonging to Christ and living to please self. Make no mistake on that point.[7]

NOBILITY

Christian women have been called to a much higher level of living than the self-focused attitudes of our day. We have been called to be noble in our demeanor and in our lives. What actually constitutes noble character? Allow me to suggest a few synonyms for the word noble: distinguished, honorable, virtuous, moral, principled, magnanimous, admirable, decent, good, honest, upright, reliable, esteemed; in short, of the highest quality.

What is God's great call on your life? Probably the closest answer to that great question would be the fusing together of all of these character traits into the inward life of a female. Isn't that what the apostle Peter meant when he wrote, "Your beauty should not come from outward adornment, such as braided hair and the wearing of gold jewelry and fine clothes. Instead, it should be that of your inner self, the unfading beauty of a gentle and quiet spirit, which is of great worth in God's sight. For this is the way the holy women of the past who put their hope in God used to make themselves beautiful…" (1 Peter 3:3-5a NIV)

Man looks upon the outward, but God sees the heart. He realizes something that many women overlook: A woman's body ends up in the ground, but the inner self—who she really is—lives forever. No wonder it is so important to cultivate godliness! No wonder the godly inner life of a woman is said to be "of great worth in God's sight."

It is that inward beauty that God has called us to personify. What a contrast there is between this mindset and that of the selfish thinking the world promotes for women. In fact, let's take a look at some synonyms of this word selfish just to deepen this sense of contrast: self-seeking, grasping, stingy, mercenary, egotistic, self-concerned, uncharitable, self-serving, self-absorbed; in short, looking out for Number One. And that last phrase perfectly describes our culture's great mantra.

How out of place are the ways of God in such a setting! Consider Judy's reflections on the painful trial she endured upon discovering her husband's involvement with pornography:

The entire tribulation of this past year has little to do with the man who crushed me because of his sexual sin. It has everything to do with me and my God. I can't see the big picture right now, but by faith I believe that this will turn out for my good and His glory. During the time of discovering his pornography I began memorizing First Peter, which has become my most precious treasure. "In this you greatly rejoice, even though now for a little while if necessary you have been distressed by various trials, that the proof of your faith, being more precious than gold, which is perishable, may be found to result in praise and glory and honor at the revelation of Jesus Christ." Amen!!

This life is not about being comfortable or "getting what we deserve" because we live good lives and serve God. This life is about being transformed into the image of Jesus. My husband is my lifetime opportunity to show the world Jesus' love. I will have to take up my cross and die to self, to my rights, to my pride, in order for the world to see Jesus. My flesh hates forgiving those who betrayed me. Jesus uttered no threats but kept entrusting Himself to Him who judges righteously. My flesh hates giving without being assured of recompense. He gave His own Blood, the Just for the unjust in order to bring me to God. Oh, the grace of God that keeps bringing errant me back to the cross time and again!

The unsaved of our culture cannot comprehend living this life of nobility because they do not understand the value of the love of God nor do they understand the power that is available.

Your marriage is the proving ground of what you really believe. Someone once said, "Marriage is a death march to a life camp." What an amazing perspective to consider! One thing is for sure: you will find out who you really are in marriage. There is nothing like this covenant, this blending of two souls into one to show you who you are at the core. I have seen the best and the worst in people after they have gotten married. I have seen plenty of people who "love the Lord" but did very un-Christlike things in their marriage, who betrayed their vows, who gave up on the one they promised to go through anything with. But I have also witnessed noble souls fight it out on their knees for lost and wayward spouses, hoping against hope and warring against principalities for the one they love. These are women who would not give up, and many to this day are fighting the fight. The contrast is palpable and being played out in the daily life of Christians even now.

What is it that causes a wife to selflessly lay down her life for the life of her husband? It is the Holy Spirit of God dwelling in us that makes all the difference in the world. It is impossible to live for someone else in the flesh; no one would even want to do such a thing. But, when you got saved you joined yourself to eternal power and love. God has not given you "a spirit of fear, but of power and of love and of a sound mind." (1 Timothy 1:7 NKJV) He has dressed you in His righteousness and given you all the spiritual tools you need to live at a higher level. All that is needed on your part is willingness to live this noble life.

For me, my defining moment came in a phone booth nearly 40 years ago. Since then I have had to live out what I consecrated myself to do that day. I haven't done it perfectly, but that has been my desire.

I had filed for divorce and run off with another man. It was then that I had a very fateful conversation with my parents who instructed me to reconsider my choices. After years of my husband's flagrant sin, God came to me and presented me with two options. I could remain as I was, with a different man in a completely new and promising relationship, or I could fling all my trust on Him and let Him live out His life through me. Of course, at the time I had no idea what that would actually mean in the long run. All I knew at the time was that God was asking me to trust Him implicitly with my whole life—which meant going back to an unfaithful husband and what surely would prove to be more crushing heartbreaks. Somehow in my very young and immature and sinful condition, I decided to put my trust in God. As it turned out it was one of the hardest decisions of my life but one of the most important decisions of my life. Not only did God restore my marriage, but the bigger and more important issue was my relationship with God. Had I decided to follow my feelings and "do what was best for me," I know I would have missed out on the priceless treasure the Lord had for me. The relationship with that man almost certainly would have ended in another heartbreak and I probably would have ended up as a miserable, selfish woman running from one relationship to another trying to heal my own brokenness.

The decision that I made that day—and that many other women have made—was not for the sake of a man or a marriage but for the living God. Our consecration was to put our lives, our happiness, our everything in His worthy hands and trust Him to unfold His plan—no matter what the cost may be. Even in this He would take responsibility, if I would just trust Him. All I can say is that the power to love the unlovable was granted; in fact, loving Steve has been the joy of my life. Forgiveness, instant and happily granted, was to be my new way of life. The Lord strengthened me to give myself unreservedly and happily to this man who continued to struggle and fail for some time. The desire and power to give my life to help him make it was my portion. And, it should be noted, that there have been many others who have made similar consecrations. None of us can take credit for any of it—it was and is God's promise to any who will believe Him—"if you lose your life for my sake you will find it." That is my testimony and I have never had a day's regret for the decision I made in that phone booth so many years ago!

Part Two

LETTERS TO
HURTING WIVES

HIS PRESENCE THROUGH PAIN

Dear Melody,

I don't mind it at all that you "dumped on me." I know what it is like to have a "bad day" while facing such "waves of pain" as you shared in your letter. You probably feel as though you're drowning in an ocean of despair with no rescue in sight. Believe me, I have been there many times in the past. I wish I would've had someone to talk to when my waves hit.

I can understand your being baffled by all your troubles, wondering "What is the point of it all?" At first glance, the option to just throw up your hands and walk away seems very appealing when you consider all the misery you're likely to suffer by staying with your husband. But, let me ask you something: what has kept you from giving up after fifteen years of grief in this marriage? What has been your motivation to hold on? I think you will agree with me that it's more than a wife's natural commitment to marriage; there must be something deeper.

It goes without saying that the Lord leads different wives to respond to their husband's sin in different ways. He often releases wives from their marriage vows who are suffering the pain of infidelity.

In your case, it seems that He has asked you to remain in the marriage. You are one of those rare people who has been able to grasp the good that God can accomplish inside you through an ordeal such as this. Perhaps you've not given up because deep in your heart you know that God is doing something very wonderful inside of you. So despite how much it hurts, you don't want to move from under the Potter's hands. I remember in one of our conversations you said to me, "As much as this hurts, I know God is purging me of stuff that He could not have gotten at in any other way." How precious those words must have been to the Lover of your soul!

The most intimate and wonderful experiences that I have ever had with the Lord happened when I was in the throes of total anguish and absolute helplessness. What a bitter-sweet existence it was during those times. Although I longed for the suffering to end, I realized when it was over that the strong sense of the Lord's nearness was diminishing. It is the joy of such closeness that drives us to seek God through pain; there is nothing quite like it. The amazing fruit that comes into our lives through the suffering is well worth the pain. Most women just want it to go away! I understand that too.

We have all heard nice sermons about God's love and faithfulness, but if it isn't worked into our hearts it just becomes more head knowledge. It is the very kind of suffering you are currently experiencing that allows the Holy Spirit to do a powerful work within a believer. God is imparting to you a knowledge of Himself which simply cannot be learned through sermons or books. He is doing a deep and precise work in your soul, carefully molding you into the image of His Son, Jesus Christ. One day you will appreciate what God has done in your inward life—even more than you would ever appreciate having a "good marriage."

The apostle Paul, who endured so much for Christ's sake, testified: "For just as the sufferings of Christ are ours in abundance, so also our comfort is abundant through Christ." (2 Corinthians 1:5) We sense the presence of God in such a powerful way when He allows us to experience pain because our sights are fixed upon the One who is able to comfort us in all our distresses.

Another major blessing in all you're going through is the way the Lord will be able to use you one day to help others who are experiencing the same thing. There is something about suffering that creates a beautiful attraction to other people in need. It will amaze you how other hurting wives will seem to come from nowhere to seek your advice. Paul was well aware that our heavenly Father "comforts us in all our affliction so that we may be able to comfort those who are in any affliction with the comfort with which we ourselves are comforted by God." (2 Corinthians 1:4)

This reminds me of the true story of Corrie and Betsy Ten Boom, two sisters who endured unspeakable suffering in a Nazi concentration camp during World War II. As Betsy was dying, she turned to Corrie and said, "We must tell them, Corrie— anyone who will listen. They will believe us because we have been there."

So, Melody, be encouraged and know that God is developing a powerful testimony in you. It is His sustaining power that is keeping you through the deepest waters. And you will discover that His love goes beyond any fleeting happiness resulting from favorable outward circumstances.

I pray that God will grant you the strength to hold onto that which now seems most painful but, in the end, will turn out to be that which best serves your soul.

DEALING WITH SUSPICIONS

Dear Janet,

Your question concerning whether or not you should confront your husband because of your suspicions is a very valid one. The first thing you must determine is if your suspicions are based on actual facts or just your own fear.

Men in sexual sin can be extremely smooth and very cunning. Most have perfected the art of deception and have led a double life for many years. Only the Lord knows the complete truth about what a man is doing in private. I have experienced both sides of the coin: living in obsessive fear—just waiting for the next devastating revelation—and trustfully watching the Lord at work.

I can remember one experience in Los Angeles before Steve came to the Lord. He worked the night shift at the jail and usually got home by 8 a.m. But on one particular morning, I called him from my job several times. Each time, I got no answer. My heart started to sink. I knew something was wrong because he was in and out of sexual sin all the time back then. It was possible that he had run an errand, but I had a feeling he was with a prostitute.

It wasn't until I got home that evening that I was able to talk to him. I didn't beat around the bush. I asked him straight out if he had been with someone else that day. Of course, he swore up and down that he hadn't, but I didn't believe him one bit. I continued to question him until finally he admitted that he had, in fact, been with a prostitute.

In those days I couldn't discern the difference between when it was God revealing something to me and when it was just my own nagging suspicions. On many occasions my hunches were wrong.

Even after Steve came to the Lord and began to change, I was still overly suspicious. I had been so hurt that it took years before I was completely free of this fear. In hindsight I can see how the devil used my fears to torment me. I conjured up all sorts of scenarios in my mind when he was alone or getting home late. Had I verbalized and acted upon all my inner fears, we would surely have ended up divorced.

My obsession with what he was doing, thinking, saying, plotting and so on only reinforced my fears. Whenever the phone rang, and I couldn't figure out whom he was talking to, I imagined it was a secret lover. Eventually, to my relief and embarrassment, it would end up being some friend of ours. My hyperactive imagination kept me in a prison of despair during this whole period. In looking back on that time I can see that I was in my own form of self-centeredness.

How do you know if your misgivings are rooted in fear and influenced by the devil or if they are based upon fact and divinely inspired? The truth is there is no sure-fire way of knowing what your husband's doing or what's in his heart. Nevertheless, there are some questions you can ask yourself which will help you navigate through some of your suspicions.

What has been your husband's track record during the last six months? Have you actually caught him in sin? Is there any evidence which definitely warrants your suspicions or do you just struggle with vague fears? For instance, has he been coming home late from work? Has money been disappearing that he can't account for? Does he give ambiguous answers or does he seem sincere? Does he still seem angry, defensive and combative or does it seem as though he is changing? How does he treat you and the kids? Is he willing to have his phone and computer filtered?

What about his walk with God? Does he seem hungry for the Lord? Does he look forward to going to church or does he look to avoid it? Does he spend time with the Lord each day? Is he reading his Bible? Does he spend hours sitting in front of the television?

It is important for the wife to walk the fine line between trust and caution. One extreme keeps a wife in ignorance while the other keeps her in a miserable life of fear.

I encourage you to use the questions listed above as a guideline to help you honestly evaluate your suspicions. If, after answering these questions, you still have nothing concrete to go on except a nagging sense that something is not right, get down on your knees before God. Deliberately put your husband in His hands. Then, ask Him to expose any secret sin that your husband might be involved in. Finally, pray that He sets you free from any life-dominating fear. Trust Him to answer your prayers.

WHY SHOULD I PUT UP WITH THIS?

Dear Lauren,

Yes, I agree that your life would probably be much easier without all of the heartache and grief of this marriage, but does having a comfortable, pain-free life mean so much to you that you would end your marriage for it? Does his pornography addiction really warrant divorce? This is a question you will ultimately have to decide for yourself. If he continues to remain in ongoing, unrepentant sin, the time may come that you will want to seek God about whether or not you should stay in this marriage. Before you get to that point however, I would like you to consider a few things.

We will all face adversity and suffering in this world, simply because this world is, for the most part, in the hands of the enemy. How we respond to that pain will, to a large extent, determine the path our lives will take with God.

For the seeking heart, there is only one response: a humble willingness to submit one's grief-stricken heart into the hands of the Heavenly Father. This response comes from the desire to be more like Jesus. It is the submission of one's entire being into the life-changing processes of the Almighty.

Having a husband in sexual sin is both painful and humbling. It helps a woman see her own need for the Lord's help in her life. It is difficult to be in that place of helplessness and pain, and yet because God is drawn to the afflicted, His presence can actually make it a glorious place. Make no mistake about it though, God uses this suffering to purify the woman of self-centeredness, self-righteousness and self-sufficiency— attitudes most of us never dreamed we had in us. Through this fiery trial her compassion for the needs of others grows and matures. The wife who has been broken like this tends to see her husband's needs, rather than his failures.

There is another response to this suffering: a bitterness which is easy to justify when one has been hurt by the sin of another. It is easy for the wife to see herself as a victim of her husband's sin. This especially becomes true when she surrounds herself with others who treat her as a victim. Of course, it is true that in a very real way the wife is a victim of her husband's sin. However, it is important for the wife to remember that—to one degree or another—every human on the planet has victimized others with their sin.

Bitterness causes a person to turn away from Jesus in the heart. Everything one does comes from the heart. How believers treat those who hurt them is an important aspect of Christianity. It should be remembered that our Savior was beaten, humiliated and murdered, and yet He never retaliated against His oppressors. Read the words of Peter regarding this subject:

> For this finds favor, if for the sake of conscience toward God a man bears up under sorrows when suffering unjustly. For what credit is there if, when you sin and are harshly treated, you endure it with patience? But if when you do what is right and suffer for it you patiently endure it, this finds favor with God.
>
> For you have been called for this purpose, since Christ also suffered for you, leaving you an example for you to follow in His steps, who committed no sin, nor was any deceit found in His mouth; and while being reviled, He did not revile in return; while suffering, He uttered no threats, but kept entrusting Himself to Him who judges righteously. (1 Peter 2:19-23)

The Lord wants to comfort the wife in her suffering and then use that suffering to help her grow to be more Christlike. But, if a woman never grows out of the place of seeing herself as a victim, nothing good will be accomplished in her life through it: she will have suffered for nothing! Instead of seeing the Lord with her through the whole ordeal, helping her, keeping her, sustaining her and molding her, all she can see is that she has been wronged by someone.

I believe that one reason God allows us to go through so much grief is so He can bring us into the light about what we are really like inside. It is all with the ultimate goal of making us more like Jesus. One illustration my husband Steve has used in the past is that of the tube of toothpaste. When you put pressure on it, the only thing that is going to come out of it is what's inside. Likewise, when affliction begins to squeeze us, what's inside is going to come out. Another illustration is that when the fire is put to the metal, the impurities rise to the top where they can be scooped off.

I believe that God is very intent on getting us to be real with Him and with ourselves. The days of superficial Christianity are coming to an end. He has to get us to look inside and see what we are really like so that we can repent and become the holy people He desires us to be.

I, too, suffered greatly at the hands of an unfaithful husband, but there came a time when I began to see beyond Steve's sin and started to recognize my own need for correction and help. Once I got a sight of that, my whole perspective changed. Now I can look back on this period of my life and can, with all sincerity, thank God for every bit of it. Why? Because this ordeal was the only way He was going to be able to help me in my own need. Before I went through this experience, my sense of need for God was very shallow, but the pain and rejection I experienced brought me to my knees and put something of depth in me that is worth everything I went through.

I realize that you have those around you who are encouraging the idea, "Why should I put up with this?" The answer to that question is twofold. First, you will endure the pain of your husband's pornography problem because you want to extend the same mercy and forgiveness to him that the Lord has extended to you. Second, you would rather allow God to use this time to mold you into the image of Christ than to run from it. I hope this letter will encourage you to "bear all things, believe all things, hope all things, endure all things. Love never fails…" (1 Corinthians 13:7-8)

THE ENCOURAGING WIFE

Dear Ann,

I appreciate so much your sincere desire to be a blessing to your husband. Life's a lot easier when you have a husband who is really trying to do what's right. The key to his living victoriously is faithfulness and endurance, staying humble before the Lord and staying in a heart of repentance. If he remains diligent and chooses to do those things God has shown him, he will make it!

Your role is to be his cheerleader, not just when he scores a touchdown, but even after he fumbles the ball! Don't ever hold his mistakes against him. As best as you can, create an atmosphere of grace for him.* Let him know that you are totally committed to him. No matter what kind of day he's had, show him that you are in his corner. His sincere desire to walk in victory will enable you to be completely supportive.

I'm glad to hear you are also being responsive to him during intimate times. Many wives punish their husbands in the bedroom by rejecting their advances.† However, what these women don't realize is that this often exacerbates the problem. Generally speaking, the more satisfied a husband is at home, the less inclined he is to search elsewhere! In First Corinthians 7:5 Paul warns married couples: "Stop depriving one another, except by agreement for a time that you may devote yourselves to prayer, and come together again lest Satan tempt you because of your lack of self-control."

Please continue to encourage your husband to have his daily time with the Lord. As you know, it is essential that you express support without nagging him. Perhaps you could even suggest that the two of you spend some time together in the Bible every evening.

---

* There is a fine line between allowing a husband to remain in sin and "creating an atmosphere of grace." This husband's attitude allows for this.

† Again, there is another side to this. There are times when abstinence is the best policy, e.g. when there is a legitimate possibility of the husband transmitting an STD.

As your husband matures in his walk with the Lord, one day he will cross a defining line—sexual sin will be completely behind him. I suspect that when that day comes he will gladly have this to say about his wife:

"Her children rise up and bless her; her husband also, he praises her, saying: 'Many daughters have done nobly, but you excel them all.' Charm is deceitful and beauty is vain, but a woman who fears the Lord, she shall be praised." (Proverbs 31:28-30)

JUST STOP IT!

Dear Jamie,

In your recent letter you asked what has become to me a very common question: "Why can't he just stop it?" For those who have not been obsessed with sex, it is hard to comprehend what is so difficult about saying "no" to sexual temptation. How can it be so hard to walk away from something so obviously laden with horrible consequences? It seems so simple—that it is only a matter of self-control. We often use such verses in the Bible as the passage you quoted to strengthen our argument: "No temptation has overtaken you but such as is common to man; and God is faithful, who will not allow you to be tempted beyond what you are able, but with the temptation will provide the way of escape also, that you may be able to endure it. Therefore, my beloved, flee from idolatry." (1 Corinthians 10:13-14)

You must understand that if it were easy for your husband to quit acting out, his problem would not be called an addiction. By definition, addictive behavior is any uncontrolled habit which is difficult to give up; such addictions almost always lead to negative consequences. Take, for example, a young prostitute living on the streets of New York City who is addicted to crack cocaine. Perhaps at one point in time she anticipated a bright future. However, over the years her life has become a vicious cycle of degradation and misery. To us, it seems so ridiculous for a woman to throw her life away like this. But that's because we don't understand the overwhelming power of the sin that has gripped her life. Or do we?

Do you have a habit of gossiping? Do you have a covetous heart? Those are "little sins" in the eyes of most, but they can be soul destroying too. We often lack compassion for others who are bound up in some sin that we've never struggled with. It is quite easy to be self-righteous and point a condemning finger at someone with a life-dominating problem.

For years I was a compulsive spendthrift. I bought clothes, housewares and anything that seemed like a bargain or a necessity. Without using much wisdom at all, I spent money frivolously and selfishly. Although covetousness is prevalent in the American Church it is rarely censured or even preached about. This just allowed me to justify my over-indulgences. Steve was bound in sexual sin, and I was hooked on wasting money on unnecessary things. In God's eyes I was a poor steward and just as unrighteous as he was—probably more so because of my horrible inability to see my own sins.

As the Apostle Paul pointed out in the Scripture passage above, the believer has the divine power available to overcome temptation. But in a practical sense, the person must learn how to appropriate that power. This typically takes time—especially for the one who has lived in deep bondage for years. We wives must resist the urge to throw Scriptures at our husband in an attempt to get them to do right.

Why doesn't your husband just stop? It sounds like he is sincerely trying to do the right thing. Change takes time. Failures can almost be expected along the way. Be patient and show him compassion. God is working in his life and it certainly seems as though he is responding. The day is approaching when he *will* stop by the grace of God! Do your utmost to believe the best and cheer him on. One day your husband will be able to testify, "my wife had a lot to do with me getting free"!

CONDEMNATION AND WORSHIP

Dear Karen,

I know just how you feel, questioning your walk with God because of the way you treat your husband at times. The Lord understands your struggle. So don't be overly hard on yourself.

All sincere believers struggle with this question: "If I really love God how can I be so ugly inside?" Self examination is a necessary part of the Christian life, but it does need to be balanced with the grace God extends to the repentant sinner. The Lord only asks that, when we hurt or offend others, that we repent to them and to God and sincerely do our best not to repeat the offense.

Your second question is also profound: "How can I worship the Lord when I'm so evil inside?" But it shows that you don't have a full understanding of your relationship with God. As Christians, we often fall prey to the misconception that we must first be completely obedient before we dare come into His presence. There is some degree of truth to this. We must never come before the Almighty's throne in a presumptuous or irreverent manner.

But our heavenly Father knows that we are human and that we often miss the mark. Nevertheless, He loves us and longs to have unbroken fellowship with us. When we worship Him from our hearts, we are united with Him spiritually.

Unfortunately, many people put the cart before the horse, so to speak. They think that they must become holy before they can be intimate with God. Not so! When we come humbly before the Lord, by His grace we are allowed entrance into His holiness, which makes us *want* to do what is right.

However, the devil tries to convince us that we must first punish ourselves before God will even hear our prayers. When we believe this blatant lie, we take upon ourselves the role of judge. Our relationship with the Lord becomes completely based upon our performance level (i.e., works). We are then the center rather than Jesus—this is precisely the devil's goal.

But the truth of the matter is that when we sincerely confess our sins He will forgive us. (1 John 1:9)

We teach the men in the Pure Life residential program to come into our chapel services ready to worship God—even if they acted like the devil himself fifteen minutes before the meeting! The best way to break free of a devilish spirit is to repent and enter into the Spirit of the Lord. Repentance not only involves us turning away from sin, but it also means that we turn toward God.

You struggle over the bitterness you feel when your husband is unfaithful to you in his heart. The best remedy to bitter water in the well is to flush it out with the Water of Life! Karen, some of my most liberating experiences occurred when I found a quiet place to shut out all of the distractions of the world, got on my knees and began to tell Jesus how much I loved Him.

Although most of my two hours with the Lord in the morning is spent in prayer and Bible study, I also try to spend time just worshiping Him. There have been times I have become so overwhelmed with God's goodness that I've ended up with my face buried in the carpet weeping. On other occasions I became so exhilarated with Him that I had to dance! I love to worship Jesus and tell Him how much I love Him and appreciate all that He's done for me.

Several wives have commented that they would express such gratitude only if their marriages were restored. But what does that say about their relationship with God? If you don't learn how to worship God and thank Him in the midst of trials, you will never do so with sincerity once they're over. The more you worship God, the more you will want to worship Him regardless of your circumstances. So when you feel like there's nowhere else to turn, you can find shelter and have fullness of joy in the presence of the Lord.

Please remember that the Lord longs to be with you, in spite of your failures. Just repent and enter in!

TOO MANY VOICES

Dear Cynthia,

It is difficult to imagine how hard it must be to have a family so against your marriage. When you married James, you entered into an exclusive relationship that no one else has any right to. You will have to be the one who establishes this fact with your family members, who apparently feel it is their place to dictate to you how you should handle your marriage.

The Lord established one of the fundamental principles of marriage when He said, "For this cause a man shall leave his father and mother, and shall cleave to his wife: they shall become one flesh." (Genesis 2:24) The same holds true for the daughter who marries.

It can be so confusing when we listen to too many voices. Everybody has an opinion about how you should handle a particular situation, and what compounds the problem is that everyone's opinion is usually different. On top of that is the fact that it is difficult for family members to be objective and supportive when they see a loved one experiencing pain.

Why does your family want you to divorce James? Sometimes well-intentioned family members don't realize that their advice is largely because they don't want to experience their own pain of seeing you hurt. On the surface it seems so loving and generous, but perhaps their emotional bond with you has blinded them to what God desires in the situation. The first person you should look to for guidance is the Lord. It is His voice you should seek to hear.

The way my parents handled my situation is a great example of what I'm trying to express. When they became aware of how Steve was hurting me, they were definitely on the side of me divorcing him. But as they began to earnestly pray for our situation, to their surprise the Lord showed them that it was His will for me to remain with Steve.

I have to say that they are the rare exception in such cases. In your situation, your parents have clearly shown they are not at the place spiritually to be able to be objective enough to hear God's voice. I encourage you to go to your pastor (or his wife) for advice. They should be spiritually mature and emotionally detached enough to help you with the kind of counsel that will look for God's will above all else. ~

FILLING THE VOID

Dear Susan,

I really appreciate how you poured your heart out in your letter. I know firsthand what it's like to pursue worthless things in order to bring momentary fulfillment. Most of us just mindlessly default to something that will fill the void in our hearts without giving it a second thought as to its consequences.

During the early years of my marriage, I wasted countless hours and spent hundreds of dollars trying to make myself feel better. Why? Well, most of the time I felt empty and alone. My life seemed meaningless. So, out of desperation I tried to fill the void through shopping. I was never satisfied with what I had. A part of almost every paycheck was spent on some new outfit. I had to have my hair and nails done frequently. Later, I was into interior decorating. I was on a mission to spruce up our home. Whenever I purchased something new, whether it was an outfit or a piece of furniture, I felt a sense of exhilaration for a couple of days. Then the feelings of emptiness would return and remain until the next shopping spree. Now, in retrospect, I see that the more I bought, the emptier I felt inside.

At the time, it never even occurred to me that I might be doing something displeasing to God. Of course, buying a new skirt is not a sin. However, in reality I had become just as obsessed with spending money as my husband was with sex. While my sin seemed innocent compared to his, both were idolatrous attempts to fill a void in our hearts meant for Jesus to occupy. Those "other things" became a substitute for my relationship with the Lord.

As I matured and came into a deeper understanding of God, He mercifully began to convict me of my excessive spending. I saw how I had turned to worldly pleasures in my pain rather than to Him. I had minimized and even justified my splurging because of all the pain my husband put me through. Nevertheless, just as it took years for him to overcome the tremendous stronghold of sexual lust, it took some time for me to break free of my own lust. It was a huge step forward for me when I admitted that what I was doing was sinful. It had been so easy to justify myself because it seemed so mild compared to what Steve was doing.

Since then, having a relationship with the Lord has become the most important thing in my life. I love my husband and never want to revisit those painful years I left behind, but the joy that fills my heart comes from what I have in God—not in the things this world has to offer—nor even in having a great marriage. I hope and pray that you also will discover the true Wellspring of all fulfillment: just Jesus, Himself.

FRUITS OF REPENTANCE

Dear Pam,

I would be glad to respond to your question, "How can I know that my husband has truly repented?" Repentance is, of course, absolutely essential to overcoming sin.

Unfortunately, many of those in sexual sin never experience true repentance. Although they may cry over their sin, plead with God to set them free, and make determined "efforts" at achieving victory, they haven't truly had the inward change of heart that brings real freedom.

I remember a couple named Bill and Fran we counseled some time ago. They had been married eight years and had two small children by the time Bill entered our residential program. He had a track record of unfaithfulness. Like so many men in sexual sin, he would seemingly do well for some time but would then go on another binge of sexual sin. Each time the tears of sorrow and promises of "I'll never do it again!" would stream forth. "I don't know why God won't set me free!" Bill would protest. "I'm doing everything I know to do to get victory," he would exclaim with a tinge of resentment toward the Lord. Fran even found herself getting angry with God because she was so convinced of her husband's sincerity.

During this whole period, Bill had led Fran to believe that his problems were limited to pornography. Eventually it came out that he had also been visiting prostitutes. As God arranged things, it was right then that she found out about Pure Life Ministries.

Immediately, Fran gave him an ultimatum. "That's it, Bill! You either go to Pure Life or we're through!" she angrily told him. Bill complied with her wishes to enter the residential program and assured the staff that he sincerely wanted help.

Generally, when a new guy comes into our program, the Pure Life counselors can quickly figure out what his problems are, how well he will get along with the others in the program and how cooperative he will be with the staff. What really takes time to discern is the actual level of his sincerity. The truth almost always comes out eventually.

It took quite some time to figure Bill out. He was a real challenge because he was so good at presenting a false image— he even had our counselors fooled for a while. But our staff understands how deceptive these men can be because they themselves have a history of sexual sin and the deception that accompanies it. They know that there are some men they just cannot figure out without the help of the Holy Spirit.

For several weeks, Bill did everything "right" in the program. He did his homework—earnestly. He did what his counselors told him to do. He listened attentively to the messages preached in our chapel services. He continually expressed a desire to mature as a Christian, but still, his great breakthrough never came. Was there a lack of motivation? Was he still clinging to some secret sin? Did he have a hidden agenda? Only time would tell.

Before long, we began suspecting that Bill's tearful bouts of repentance were insincere. Then one day we found out that he had been flirting with a woman at his job. It became clear to the staff that, despite all of his protests to the contrary, he simply wasn't truly repenting of his sin. He had been willing to obey God to a certain extent but balked when God started asking for a full surrender.

A man's sincerity level is much more difficult to ascertain when he is at home. It takes some men time to come out of the clutches of sexual sin. But I am convinced that there isn't a sincere man alive who couldn't overcome his sin at the Pure Life residential program. I say this because everything he needs to find victory is made available to him: counselors with their own testimony of victory, tight accountability and most of all, a godly environment where life-changing repentance is commonplace.

Bill's insincerity became obvious after Fran served him his divorce papers and he quit the residential program. There was no longer a reason for him to continue the charade.

Repentance often comes in stages. A man who has been deeply entrenched in sexual sin will have years of ingrained habits to face. He will struggle with feelings of hopelessness, which can paralyze even the best of intentions. All of this is in addition to the great love he has had for his sin. But, nevertheless, if he is sincere, changes will begin to occur as he is given new direction and real hope through Jesus Christ.

We encourage wives to look for *fruits* of repentance, as John the Baptist called them. There should be some evidence that genuine effort is being put forth. Once your husband sets himself on the right course to victory—walking in daily repentance, spending time in the Word and in prayer, staying accountable and loving others (especially his wife)—God will take him across a line. The day will come when God will get him to a place spiritually where he can make that final surrender and consecration, and he will do it.

The fruits of repentance are positive indicators that a real heart transformation is underway. Watch for them, and you will get a better idea of your husband's level of commitment.

CONFRONTING THE HUSBAND

Dear Joyce,

Perhaps it's time to confront your husband. His persistence in viewing pornography and then lying about it warrants your taking some serious action.

In Matthew 18, Jesus lays out the framework for proper biblical confrontation. He said, "And if your brother sins, go and reprove him in private; if he listens to you, you have won your brother. But if he does not listen to you, take one or two more with you, so that by the mouth of two or three witnesses every fact may be confirmed. And if he refuses to listen to them, tell it to the church; and if he refuses to listen even to the church, let him be to you as a Gentile and a tax-gatherer." (Matthew 18:15-17)

You shared in your letter that you had tried, on three separate occasions, to have serious talks with Pete about his problem. Each time he reacted defensively. In the words of Jesus, he didn't "listen to you."

So now your next step is to approach him with one or two other believers. For starters, I suggest that you make an appointment with your pastor. Explain to him your situation and ask him to speak with your husband. I only say this because your husband attends church and considers himself a Christian.

If your pastor is unwilling to get involved, don't give up! Search for a godly person you both respect, perhaps a close friend or an elder of the church.

More than likely your husband will become angry and see this as an invasion of privacy. No doubt such exposure will be humiliating to him. At any rate, it is important for you to be strong and compassionate through the whole ordeal. As you prepare to do this, you will face a strong temptation to call the whole thing off. Resist it! You will do him a tremendous disservice if you continue to ignore his hypocrisy. If his wife won't love him enough to confront him, who will?

Don't feel guilty for bringing others into this. It would truly be unmerciful on your part if you cover up for him and pretend that everything is fine. Again, he may get upset with you, but that's all right. I don't mean to be insensitive, but he will get over it. Joyce, you must keep a proper perspective: your husband's soul could be at stake here. A severe blow to his pride is one of his greatest needs, and his hurt feelings are only a minor consequence in the whole scheme of things.

You see, you cannot allow him to use anger or resentment to dominate the situation. For his sake, you must remain rational and be firm with him no matter how he responds. This way you have a better chance at salvaging your marriage. Let's pray that your husband will WAKE UP out of the delusion that he can participate in such darkness and still think that he's walking with the Lord.

As far as a separation is concerned, I advise you to try this kind of confrontation first before you take that step. It would not be wise to threaten him with a separation, unless you are prepared to follow through and accept all the ramifications this would entail. However, if nothing changes after your pastor becomes involved, separation may be the best course of action.

I will be praying for you and hope that the Lord will open Pete's eyes.

I FEEL LIKE I'M LOSING MY MIND!

Dear Anna,

You have beautifully articulated the agony of countless women: "Is my husband a liar, or am I just imagining all of this? I don't know what to believe anymore. I feel like I'm losing my mind!"

From what you expressed in your letter, it is obvious that your husband is manipulating you. You mentioned that every time you attempt to discuss his problems with him, he somehow twists the whole conversation around and makes you the focal point of the discussion, rather than him. You also said that when you confront him with undeniable evidence about his unfaithfulness, he manages to get everything so confused that you "don't know up from down."

Let me tell you: I've been there and done that! I experienced the same thing with Steve. Whenever I tried to talk to him about his sexual sin or the way he was treating me, he would cleverly commandeer the conversation and somehow get the focus on me. To this day, I don't know exactly how he did it. Each time, at the end of our discussion, I felt like I had made a big deal about nothing or that I was only imagining things. So masterful was he at manipulating me that I would actually end up being the one to repent!

One of the reasons he got away with this was because I desperately wanted to believe the best about my husband. He used his strong, domineering personality to emotionally bully me into submission.

As it turned out, my suspicions were right on target. Eventually I came to the realization that trying to convince Steve to do the right thing was a hopeless cause. It was then I decided to leave him. I simply couldn't continue to accept his lies, his manipulation and his sleeping around. I knew that he would never change as long as he was allowed to stay in control of the situation. I hoped my leaving would cause him to see things right, but there were no guarantees.

Anna, you must be strong and take a firm stand in your dealings with Tony in the future. It's obvious from what you shared in your letter that he is being unfaithful to you. Since he isn't sincerely responding to your discussions, you may need to consider a separation. It could be the very jolt he needs! Just be careful not to get into your own form of manipulation. Ask the Lord to give you the wisdom to do what is right and the strength to follow through with whatever He lays on your heart.

THE ABUSIVE HUSBAND

Dear Elaine,

It sounds as though you and your kids are in an extremely volatile situation. Not only is your husband addicted to pornography, insanely jealous and very controlling, but he is physically and emotionally abusive.

The key word here is CONTROL. Your husband is using his temper to manipulate and control you. You are emotionally beaten down and thoroughly intimidated by him.

Elaine, many women stay in unhealthy relationships, like yours. They develop an emotional dependence on their husbands that, believe it or not, is only strengthened by the sense that they cannot win his affections. In fact, the more disapproval these women sense through his anger, the more motivated they become to win back the approval that they've lost. Eventually they come to see this unhealthy relationship as normal.

I know that because you are "weak" by nature you feel that you have to stay. He has hammered on your emotions for so long you have come to believe you can't make it without him. Well, Elaine, I know a letter cannot impart the strength you need, but perhaps I can offer some helpful advice.

You must first take control of the situation. I know the thought of that seems overwhelming to you, because once he starts yelling, you have always wilted. But you must see that *you* are allowing your husband to control you with his anger. This keeps you beaten down and unable to take a stand. And as long as he is in control, it is highly unlikely that he will feel motivated to earnestly seek God for his deliverance.

I believe your circumstances are severe enough to warrant an immediate separation from him as well as a restraining order. If you are fearful of him because of his violent, controlling nature, I suggest that you take the kids and leave when he's at work. (You might want to check with an attorney or an advocate at your local women's shelter before pursuing this course of action.)

Once you've left, be aware of the fact that you will naturally start to crave his affection and attention again. You will probably second-guess your decision to leave. An overwhelming sense of insecurity may rise up within you. This may prompt you to remember his positive side or even reminisce about your happiest moments with him. Meanwhile, your memory of his abusiveness will fade. If you feel an overwhelming temptation to contact him "just to see how he's doing," resist it! Don't be caught off guard! The less contact the better.

You should also be aware of the fact that you will probably feel a sense of guilt over leaving him. That's okay—he'll be fine without you. It is important that you remember that he has caused this separation, not you. You are now in the driver's seat—don't give it up. You must call the shots.

When you do eventually speak to him, you must control the conversation. Don't talk to him if he is in a rage, and don't let him sweet-talk you into coming home right away. Remember: he's a controller and will use every angle possible in order to get his own way. Just cut him off and keep the conversation strictly business (i.e. controlled visits with the kids, bills, etc.). Once you have left and are getting re-established, you will have control of the situation. *Don't give it up!*

In time, if he truly repents and turns to the Lord, his frantic efforts to get you back will be replaced with a new passion for Jesus. This is what you're looking for: "fruits of repentance." Do not be easily swayed by tears and promises. What you need to see is a change in his attitudes and his need to control you and, most of all, a life in God that seems legitimate. And you need to see this walked out for a period of time.

I am not suggesting divorce, but I do feel that it isn't safe for you or the kids to stay with your husband the way he is now. The key is for you to stay turned to the Lord through the entire process. Only He can give you the strength you need to stay free of this unhealthy relationship. And also, with you out of the way, God will have a better chance at reaching your husband's heart.

If he does have a spiritual breakthrough, perhaps you can find a good biblical counselor to help you navigate your way to reconciliation. Much work must be done in both of you for this relationship to become one that is biblically-based and God-centered.

Whatever may happen with the relationship, I just want to encourage you to seek God's face like never before. The deepening of that connection with the Lord will do more to heal your emotions than anything else. ∽

VAGUE SUSPICIONS

Dear Laura,

You shouldn't be surprised to be feeling nagging suspicions. You have been through a lot with your husband. Over a long period of time he had several affairs, was involved in all types of perversion and kept it completely hidden until you caught him. Your lack of trust for him is warranted, but I think I can share some things that will help you.

First, because you've been deeply hurt by his behavior, you will naturally tend to imagine the worse-case scenario. If you allow your mind to run wild, you will imagine him to be with another woman every time he's away from home. Realize that just because such thoughts come into your mind doesn't mean that they're legitimate.

Second, you mentioned that your husband has kept a good track record ever since he repented. There is no indication that he's been unfaithful to you in quite a while. He's been honest about his failures. He continues to press into God. You no longer see him leering at women when you're together. Although he still has his struggles from time to time, it sounds like he's doing great overall.

Third, you must remember that there is an active agent involved in your situation who wishes to sabotage your marriage: the devil. He is known as "the accuser of the brethren" and delights in planting accusatory thoughts in a wife's mind about her husband. Look for him to bring to your mind memories of past painful experiences in an attempt to torment you and cause division. Your own natural suspicions and the devil's influence will convince you that all his efforts are just more deception.

Therefore, it's very important that you constantly guard your thought life. Through this process of bringing every thought captive you will learn a little of the enormous difficulty your husband is having in keeping a pure mind. You will see how easy it is to default to natural thinking. I know how easy it is to sit and imagine the worst—it requires no effort at all to think that way. But living inside you is the Holy Spirit of God who enables you to believe the best. This requires much discipline on your part. You must do your best to control your thoughts, just like your husband must. The fact is that fear can drive a person into self-centeredness every bit as much as lust can.

The best way to avoid being dominated by fear is to pray instead of think! When those dark, sneaking suspicions start to invade your mind, begin interceding for your husband. If you will practice this, gradually you will become increasingly less susceptible to those tormenting fears. Furthermore, your prayers will help your husband attain real victory. The loser will be the devil who will grow discouraged and flee from you since his accusations will serve only to stimulate your prayer life! ⁓

ABANDONED BY GOD

Dear Shirley,

I received your letter about a week ago and have been praying about how to respond to it. I can relate to your feeling that God has abandoned you. I don't endorse it by any means, but I do understand it because I went through the same thing.

Let me briefly share with you my own testimony. My number one question for many years was: Why did God let me marry this guy when He knew what he was like? Not only did He allow me to marry Steve, He actually led me to do it! God knew beforehand all of the horrible grief I would eventually suffer in my marriage. Why didn't He cover me and shield me from it all?

It would have been very easy for me to be mad at God, considering the fact that this was my second marriage that seemed destined for divorce court. I was oblivious to the future plans and purposes of God concerning Steve and me. All I could foresee was a trail of tears and endless suffering.

There is a similar story of infidelity in the Bible. I'm referring to Hosea and Gomer. Hosea was also told by God to marry someone who would prove to be unfaithful: "Go, take to yourself a wife of harlotry." (Hosea 1:2) He obeyed the Lord and had to bear her unfaithfulness for years, but God had a bigger plan in mind.

What if I wouldn't have married Steve? Yes, such a choice would have saved me a lot of grief with him, but who's to say I would have ended up in a situation any less painful? Not only that, I would have missed the eternal work God desired to do in me through the experience.

Shirley, I don't know what was involved in your decision to marry your husband. Was it God's will for you to marry such a man because He has a bigger purpose in mind that you aren't yet seeing? Or is it possible that you pushed through your own will without waiting for a clear sense from the Lord? I don't know the answers to those questions. In one sense it doesn't really matter whether you are reaping the consequences of a poor decision or have been in the center of God's will all along. His love for you has not changed, and He will do everything possible to accomplish the most good for you through it.

Whatever happens in your situation, Shirley, know that your heavenly Father is right there with you. He will *never* abandon you and will always give you the grace to endure any suffering He allows in your life. Just purpose in your heart to seek His face like never before. Not only will you find comfort and strength in your times of weakness, but you will discover that God's grace is truly sufficient for you.

BEARING THE BURDEN

Dear Clara,

I can certainly empathize with your feeling as if you're weighed down under a thousand pounds. Having a husband who is addicted to sex can be an enormous burden.

As a wife and mother, I know you feel obligated to be the spiritual leader of the home, especially since your husband will not assume that role. Consequently, the welfare of the entire family rests upon your shoulders. Some husbands are rendered so helpless by their sin that they give up all responsibility to the family. Ultimately it is the wife who must carry the load as well as deal with her own pain, fear and emotional needs.

The psalmist said, "Cast your burden upon the Lord, and He will sustain you; He will never allow the righteous to be shaken." (Psalm 55:22) He also said, "Blessed be the Lord, who daily bears our burden, the God who is our salvation." (Psalm 68:19)

The key to allowing the Lord to be your Burden-Bearer is to stay in fellowship with Him. If you are learning to abide in the presence of Jesus, He will grant you the grace which will make your burdens lighter. Of course, this means you must make time to be with Him—even though you are holding down a job and taking care of the household. As the old hymn goes, "Oh what needless pain we bear, all because we do not carry everything to God in prayer."

A good illustration of this is found in the story of Mary and Martha found in Luke 10. There was Martha in a frenzy, anxiously running about trying to keep things together while her sister sat at the Master's feet. Jesus said to her, "Martha, Martha, you are worried and bothered about so many things; but only a few things are necessary, really only one, for Mary has chosen the good part, which shall not be taken away from her." Your situation is different, yet the principle here still applies.

Sometimes it seems so difficult to sit at His feet when you feel overwhelmed by problems. The alternative, though, is to carry that weight by yourself. It is a wife's calling to battle through spiritually for her husband, but it can only be done on her knees before the Lord.

With all the emotional and spiritual weight you are already bearing, it may seem like maintaining a vibrant devotional life is just one more thing added to the burden. All I can tell you is that if you don't have a regular prayer time, you will probably go through life feeling frustrated and defeated and you will probably make bad decisions. If you do carve out time to be with the Lord, He will be able to increase His power and grace in your life.

Pray earnestly for your husband, and then do your best to leave the worries at God's throne. As you learn to do this, you will become like Mary, finding the joy of the Lord's presence in the midst of your storm. ⌒

INTERCESSION FOR THE HUSBAND

Dear Jerry,

You asked, "How should I pray for my husband?" What a wonderful question! No doubt, it comes from the desire to see him set free of his sexual sin. I admire you for your willingness to lay down your life for Lou in this way. I would like to give you practical, everyday prayers to pray for him, but first let me share with you some principles of prayer.

Throughout Steve's period of coming out of sin, my prayer life mainly consisted of what I will call "hope-so prayers." In other words, they weren't based upon a real faith and trust in God; I just sort of threw them up to heaven, hoping that God would eventually answer them. They were, to a large extent, prayers based on a foundation of fear.

Later, I came to realize that what matters most isn't so much the number of prayers or even their fervency necessarily, but the degree of faith which accompanies them. James said, "The effective prayer of a righteous man can accomplish much." (James 5:16) What makes a believer righteous? Over and over again in Scripture we are told that it is faith that gets God's attention. Perhaps we could state it like this: the person who prays with the sense that God wants to answer those prayers can accomplish much.

What is this faith in? Is it in our ability to offer up eloquent petitions to God? Is it in our ability to exercise great mental self-control, refusing to allow any doubts to lodge in our minds? Is it in our ability to pray with a lot of passion which somehow pushes a reluctant God to do something He really doesn't want to do? No, our faith is in God's character, who He is, what He's like, what we can expect from Him regardless of what we face in our lives. Someone said, "Prayer is not overcoming God's reluctance but laying hold of His highest willingness." What a beautiful truth!

Daniel, a man of great faith, prayed the following prayer:

Alas, O Lord, the great and awesome God, who keeps
His covenant and lovingkindness for those who love
Him and keep His commandments, we have sinned,
committed iniquity, acted wickedly, and rebelled,
even turning aside from Your commandments and
ordinances....To the Lord our God belong compassion
and forgiveness, for we have rebelled against Him; nor
have we obeyed the voice of the Lord our God, to walk
in His teachings which He set before us through His
servants the prophets....

So now, our God, listen to the prayer of Your
servant and to his supplications, and for Your sake, O
Lord, let Your face shine on Your desolate sanctuary.
O my God, incline Your ear and hear! Open Your
eyes and see our desolations and the city which is
called by Your name; for we are not presenting our
supplications before You on account of any merits of
our own, but on account of Your great compassion. O
Lord, hear! O Lord, forgive! O Lord, listen and take
action! For Your own sake, O my God, do not delay,
because Your city and Your people are called by Your
name. (Daniel 9:4-19)

This prayer gives every indication that this man knew God
intimately. He knew the Lord to be merciful, compassionate
and quick to forgive. Therefore, it was to the Lord's character
that Daniel appealed. We should do the same whenever we
pray for our husbands. When we rely upon the God of all
mercy, then our faith will rise as we pray because He is a good
God who desires to save.

What empowers our prayers is the knowledge of God's
good and merciful character and a realization that the daily

activity of heaven is mercy. The atmosphere of heaven is pure, all-consuming love.

The wonderful thing about prayer that is centered in God's character is that our focus stays fixed upon Him. As we sit in His presence, His atmosphere of love invades our space. Bowed before His Majesty, we are likely to spend more time simply worshiping Him for who He is rather than fixing our eyes upon ourselves or what we want Him to do for us. As Jesus said, "…your Father knows what you need, before you ask Him." (Matthew 6:8)

If you learn to pray like this, He will begin to change your nature to match His own. Sitting in the wonder of this God of love, mercy and compassion will put you in the same Spirit He is in. Having the mind and heart of God for other people is the most effective way to help them. Before long, you will begin to feel the love of Christ for others, especially for your husband. The more God's love shapes your prayers, the more power there is in those prayers. Praying for your husband isn't a matter of convincing a reluctant God that He needs to do your husband a favor. It is appropriating the power of God through faith in Him to meet your husband's needs.

So, in light of everything I've just shared with you, allow me to make some practical suggestions concerning your daily devotions. I usually begin my time with the Lord in the Bible. Reading Scripture helps to align our minds with God's way of thinking. I also try to spend some time worshiping the Lord. There is no better way to create a heavenly atmosphere in your heart.

After time in the Word and in worship, you will be in a better frame of mind to approach the throne of the Almighty with your petitions. No doubt you may have many things and people to pray for, but I would like to present some examples of words you can say to God on your husband's behalf. These phrases aren't meant to be prayed as though there is some power in the words themselves. They are only meant to provoke you to seek the Lord for your husband in faith.

Lord, there is nothing I can do to save my husband. I believe that You are good and merciful and desire to bring my husband to victory. I appeal to Your lovingkindness to help him in his great need.

Break the power of darkness over my husband's life. Break the power that sexual pleasure has over him. Make all flesh repulsive to him, except the flesh of his wife. Give him the gift of repentance. Put a hedge of protection around him. Make every illicit sexual experience he has seem empty and futile. Take away the importance sex has in his life. Diminish his sense of need for illicit sexual behavior. Break the strong back of pride and replace it with a spirit of humility.

Help him to make a full consecration to you, O Lord. Increase His desire for the things of God. Give him a sight of Calvary and all that the cross means. Fill him with the Spirit of holiness. Give him a hunger and thirst for righteousness. Give him the peace of God which is completeness in Christ. Meet the deepest needs of his heart, Lord. Fill the void of his heart with Yourself.

Make the mercy of God real to Him and the blood of Jesus his very life. Give him a heart of compassion for the people he takes advantage of in his mind. Give him a grateful heart, Lord. Give him the desire to lay down his life for his wife and family. Bless our marriage bed, O Lord. Make our times together fulfilling to both of us. I entrust him to You, O God, and I believe You to do everything possible to save his soul and bring him to completeness in Christ.

I hope these petitions give you a little more direction in your prayer life. There is no perfect formula that God responds to—it's only faith that pleases Him. Be patient, wait, pray and believe!

WHEN THE WICKED PROSPER

Dear Lucy,

I'm so sorry to hear that your husband has divorced you and run off with another woman. News of the romantic exhilaration they are currently basking in must be crushing to you as everything in your life now seems to be crashing down around you. I can understand why you feel like God is blessing them and cursing you.* They are both making good money, going to church and living a prosperous life, seemingly without any troubles. All the while your life is full of troubles. Your job hardly pays you enough to get by. The engine in your car must be rebuilt. You feel so alone.

Lucy, has it ever occurred to you that these two may not even know the Lord? I realize they attend church, but their conduct does not reflect the life of a true believer. Having everything going well is not necessarily a sign of God's blessing on one's life. In fact, in a case like this especially, it seems more like a sign of the lack of God's hand being on their lives; either that or He has simply given them over to pursue their own lusts.

Look at your life in comparison. What I see is a sincere believer, struggling to keep her life together and remain faithful to the Lord in the midst of grief and adversity. I have experienced much of this in my relationship with God—only to discover each time that He was using these difficulties to mature my faith and draw me closer to Himself.

I don't know enough about this situation to make any real judgments. But it appears to me that these two are going their own way, without the slightest concern about what God thinks, while you, on the other hand, are being refined in the furnace of affliction.

Don't let their outward "happiness" fool you, Lucy. Happiness based on favorable circumstances is only an inch deep. David once wrote, "Do not fret because of evildoers, be

---

* This is an age-old struggle with believers (cf. Psalm 73, Habakkuk 1-3).

not envious toward wrongdoers." (Psalm 37:1) One day, they will have to face the consequences of their actions, whether it be here on earth or standing before a holy God.

The wonderful news for you is that God loves you and is intimately and intricately involved in every aspect of your life. It may seem that He is far away during times like these, but believe me, He has never been closer. Put your ex-husband in His hands and turn to Him for the comfort that only He can give you. ✑

THE FAILING HUSBAND

Dear Veronica,

Although it may be difficult for you to see it now, you are blessed to have Stan for a husband—struggles and all! I say this because he is earnestly pursuing God and refuses to give up.

You asked, "How can such a good husband and father, who spends quality time with the Lord every day, continue to struggle with something so filthy as pornography?"

Stan is a sinner, like all of us, who has grown up in a culture in which sexual perversion has almost become the norm. From childhood men are bombarded with the message that having sex is the ultimate form of pleasure and pleasure is the reason for life. I'm not at all shocked that so many men are addicted to pornography in America today—even Christian men.

Because your husband is doing all of the right things— being open with you, repenting, spending time with the Lord each day and staying accountable—there is no need to worry or fear that your marriage will take a turn for the worse. No doubt, it will take some time before he puts this struggle behind him for good. You must be patient with him as he outgrows his obsession with sex. His occasional slips are painful setbacks, but somehow the Lord is faithful to use them for good in the life of a sincere believer. Stan has demonstrated that he wants to break free from sexual sin and that he desires intimacy with the Lord. So, there is a lot of hope for the two of you!

I can remember when Steve got serious about overcoming his sin. It really hurt whenever he gave over to some temptation, but all along, those failures were actually working in our favor. Each time he blew it, his hatred for his sin deepened, and his desire to be free deepened. Eventually, he reached a point where he began to truly count the cost and make a conscious choice to resist the temptations he faced.

It sounds like Stan is in the same place Steve was in just before he crossed the line into real victory. Be encouraged! Stan is a fighter, and by God's grace he will make it! ⁓

THE UNWILLING WIFE

Dear Margaret,

I'm so sorry to hear that Jeff filed for divorce. I know our last meeting with you was very hard. It was best not to allow the counseling to continue because it didn't seem as though you were open. You felt that your marriage problems were all Jeff's fault and you didn't need to change.

Perhaps, now that Jeff is gone, you will be more open to what Steve and I have been trying to say to you.* From the first time we counseled you, we sensed that you saw yourself as a victim of Jeff's sin. There is some truth to that, of course, since he was involved in sexual sin. I never want to discount how painful it can be to go through something like this.

However, one major obstacle we found to be detrimental to Jeff's progress was how negative and unmerciful you were toward him. You demanded that he walk a straight line of perfection, unwilling to show patience or be supportive and loving to him. It was virtually impossible for him to live up to your high expectations. As we attempted to counsel him and show him the way out, time and again we felt as though our efforts to help him were being thwarted at home by your cynicism and accusations.

Another thing that was regrettable was your decision not to be intimate with him. It underscored your unwillingness to believe in him.

Whenever I tried to discuss these things with you in our counseling sessions, the conversation always shifted from talking about your life to listing all the offenses Jeff had committed that week. Also, not satisfied with his failures, you continually brought unsubstantiated accusations against him. You were bent on building a case against your husband and became so paranoid that we were unable to reason with you.

---

* This situation is not the norm; however, it points out the importance of the wife having a humble attitude with God. This was one of those situations where the wife's attitude needed to change or there would be no hope for the marriage.

It seemed clear to us that Jeff had genuinely repented of his pornography addiction. He admitted that he still struggled with looking at women in public and came to us for help—voluntarily! But you treated him with the severity due a husband who is going out with prostitutes and has no intention of changing. As a result he grew discouraged and felt as though he could never meet your demands. Yes, he failed in some areas, but you treated him as though he were a loser who would never get it together. You cannot treat a man that way and expect him to stay.†

I feel bad for you, Margaret, not only because your heart is broken over this divorce, but mostly because it sounds like you still think of yourself as the only victim in this situation. The sad fact is that due to your bitterness and resentment you have chosen a path of misery and unhappiness which will remain unaltered until you repent.

I must admit that I am puzzled over your desire to see the marriage restored. What is there to restore? If Jeff is "the same ole creep" he ever was, why would you want to go back with him?

I do not believe you can be restored to Jeff until you are first restored to God. That will only happen when you come to realize that you, too, are a sinner in desperate need of the grace of God. When you get a real sight of Calvary, the place where the Innocent One laid down His life for your sins, then you will be ready to fall to your knees humbled and broken before the Lord.

Jesus once told the story of two men who went to the temple to pray. (Luke 18:9-14) One saw himself as a filthy sinner, unworthy even to look up to God. The other saw himself as someone walking in tremendous spirituality, far beyond others around him. Jesus said that only one of these men left the temple justified in the sight of God.

---

† Of course, I don't mean to justify his decision to seek a divorce.

Margaret, your future with God depends upon which of these two attitudes you take into His throne room. If you humble yourself and repent, I'm sure that there is not only hope for this marriage to be restored, but a bright hope for your future happiness as well.

THE UNREPENTANT HUSBAND

Dear Sue,

Thanks for your note. I appreciate your openness and honesty. I know you have suffered so much from Gil's frequent acts of adultery and his unwillingness to change. The fact that he has been visiting prostitutes for the entire length of your marriage is heartbreaking.

I admit that most women would not put up with what you have had to deal with. It would be easy to grow angry and very bitter. But God, who specializes in heart surgery, will use His razor-sharp scalpel to remove from your heart any evidence of cancer because of His great love for you. He will not allow bitterness to eat away your soul as long as you keep turning to Him.

I have to say that your situation is rather unique. It is very unusual that a man will be honest about his sin if he isn't sincere about getting help. But Gil has had a track record of feeling conviction, confessing his sin with his mouth, but refusing to let it go.

True repentance is the key to breaking the cycle. What good is it to be honest if you don't repent? None, whatsoever! I tend to think that admitting his sin gives Gil some kind of temporary relief from the tremendous guilt he probably feels. Perhaps in some convoluted way he convinces himself that he is sincere in his efforts because he voluntarily tells on himself. But true repentance translates into changed behavior. However, this never seems to happen for him.

I fear that Gil may be headed for (or perhaps has already crossed) the point where God will give him completely over to his degrading passions. If that has truly happened, then he has placed himself beyond the reach of the Holy Spirit's conviction. Another possibility is that Gil has never experienced a true conversion to Christ. He may have simply learned how to play the part of Christianity outwardly without ever having truly received a regenerated heart. That would certainly explain the lack of true repentance.

I am concerned that one of Gil's biggest hindrances has been that he is a "nice guy" which makes it easy for him to convince himself that he is right with God. People with pleasant natures are very susceptible to this kind of delusion.

As far as whether or not you should separate from him, all I can say is that this is probably the most clear-cut case for biblical divorce that I have ever seen. Hopefully your pastor can get involved and help you work through the logistics of leaving Gil.

I realize that you haven't always handled everything perfectly, but the way you have stuck it out with him is nothing short of impressive. Your filing for divorce could be the thing that finally shakes him out of his complacency. If not, then my hope is that you can get on with your life in God with the true sense that you did everything possible to make it work.

THE ADULTEROUS WIFE

Dear Stacey,

Do you really believe it would help your marriage (or you) to do to your husband what he has done to you? You are very hurt right now, but I think you know better than to believe that "paying your husband back" by committing adultery is really the thing to do. The feeling of "being wanted" would offer nothing more than a temporary and empty thrill.

I can remember so well being twenty-two years old, hurting and brokenhearted. I was very vulnerable because I wasn't turning to the Lord for my comfort and help. Of course, the devil was only too happy to supply an alternative source of comfort, which came in the form of a man who appeared to be a caring Christian. He quickly sensed how naïve and vulnerable I was when we met. I didn't realize it at the time, but I was a walking target for someone like him. Foolishly, I allowed my emotions to run away with me. Before I knew what had happened, I was whisked away in an adulterous relationship that seemed to promise the world.

What I really needed at that time was a godly Christian woman who could sit me down and talk some sense into me. Unfortunately, I made many unwise decisions. Oh, if I could only share with you how deeply I came to regret some of those decisions!

Stacey, you too are very vulnerable right now. If you don't turn to the Lord, the devil will set you up just like he did to me years ago. Some guy, posing as Prince Charming, will suddenly appear in your life. You will miss the little red flags that should warn you as to what this guy is really like. For instance, what kind of "Christian" man would want to be involved with a married woman? Let's be honest: there is only one thing he is after, the very thing you are trying to escape!

Trying to find relief through some carnal method will only lead to more problems and heartaches. You will find yourself caught in a vicious cycle of sin, shame and fear that will become increasingly more difficult to escape. Believe it or not, you are at a crossroad right now. The wrong decision could literally ruin the rest of your life.

What I would suggest to you, now, is to try to calm yourself down. Why not spend some time meditating in the Psalms? I know it doesn't seem as though it would do anything to improve your situation, but it will help put you into the mindset of the Lord. The praise and adoration of the Lord conveyed in the Psalms can really help to bring you into an atmosphere of peace and comfort. The Word of God restores the soul and the mind. (Psalm 19:7)

Next, make an appointment with your pastor's wife or another godly woman. It would do you a lot of good to have someone like that intimately involved in your life right now.* I realize it may be embarrassing to confess your struggles, but they will understand. More importantly, it will bring your temptations out into the light where mature Christians will be able to help you to deal with and overcome them.

Stacey, I'm grateful you had the courage to open up with me about what is going on in your heart. You can tie up the loose ends now by taking this to someone who can help. This is a black storm, but it will pass. I'm so glad you haven't made decisions in the midst of that storm that you would later regret. We will pray that God will supply you with the needed strength to get through this painful and difficult time.

---

* Another alternative would be to go through Pure Life's At-Home Program for Wives.

MY SEXUAL NEEDS

Dear Darlene,

You are right; there are no easy answers to your problem. Your husband's lack of interest in you sexually makes his interest in homosexual pornography all the harder to handle emotionally.

Many men don't realize that women have needs which are just as real as theirs. It may be true that a woman doesn't have the hormonal build-up that a man has; however, a woman's emotional needs—which require some degree of real intimacy—more than make up for the other.

Having said that, I'm concerned about the direction your life is taking. You don't seem to be turning to the Lord in this situation. In fact, you admitted to becoming increasingly obsessed with romance novels and sensual "reality" shows on television. I think you would agree that the romantic fantasies they inspire in you are only increasing the sense of alienation you have experienced with Jimmy.

What should you do about the lack of intimacy with your husband? Since you are the one who is looking to bring about change in the marriage, it will have to start with you. The first thing I would say is that you must swear off watching those romance-driven programs on TV and get rid of the romance novels. You might ask yourself, "How are my romantic fantasies any different than Jimmy's sexual fantasies?" You need to repent as much as he does.

Second, I want to encourage you to establish a solid devotional life. Why not get involved in some good Bible studies? You might consider doing inductive studies (produced by Precept Ministries) or getting one of my husband's Bible studies (the *Walk Series*). Of course, you must establish a quality prayer life as well. You will find that getting your heart right with the Lord will fill the emptiness you feel more than anything else. Your problems will be much more manageable in His awesome presence.

Jesus is your husband, Darlene, and He knows your needs. I know there are many who consider this kind of teaching to be unrealistic or perhaps, even naïve. All I can say is that perspective comes from human logic. God's power to do good, on behalf of the one who comes to Him, is far greater than our problems. However, I have found that many women simply don't have that degree of trust in the Lord and are unwilling to put their faith in Him. My testimony to you is that when a wife really turns to God in trust, He never fails or disappoints her.

ACCOUNTABILITY

Dear Deanna,

I will offer you some helpful guidelines for holding your husband accountable, but are you sure you can handle it? If he tells you that he visited a porn site after work and masturbated, how will you react? If he tells you he is having a struggle with a girl at his job, what will you do? If he tells you he is having homosexual fantasies, will you still respect him? Once he begins baring his soul, you may find yourself devastated.

It has been our experience that it is better for the wife to take a limited role in her husband's accountability. The two of them should sit down together and lay out a plan of action that they both agree to.

There are certain areas of the sex addict's life that every wife should be involved in. First, he should keep you well-informed about what he is doing when he isn't at work. Never underestimate the cunning of a man who wants his sin. If your husband has set hours of work at a specific location, staying on top of his activities shouldn't be too difficult. It can be more challenging if he has a job that provides a lot of freedom (i.e., outside sales, driving truck, working on computers, etc.). Setting priorities is of utmost importance. If your husband has this kind of freedom and continues to struggle, you must ask yourselves if it is really worth it for him to keep his job. However, if, for some reason, there simply is no alternative, then the next best thing you can do is to agree that every night you will look him in the eye and ask him how he did that day. Knowing he will have to face that encounter may help him when he faces temptation. However, this system does not usually work smoothly, because it tends to create friction between spouses.

Another area of his life that you should be involved in is his devotional life. This means that you must be absolutely committed to meeting with God daily yourself. One thing that helps get the habit established is a structured Bible study. There are many available. You might consider *The Walk of Repentance*, which was written by my husband with the sexual addict and the hurting wife in mind. It is a 24-week Bible study. It facilitates a regimen of consistent prayer time as well.

Another thing that you should be involved in is his "screen time," whether that be watching television, using the computer, playing video games or other activities on his smartphone. We, of course, highly recommend that couples simply disconnect from cable or satellite television. It would be better to purchase televisions programs (by the season) or appropriate movies online than to subject yourselves to programming you cannot control. Pick shows together that you agree would be comparatively "safe." Plan your times to watch movies or television, rather than simply turning it on every night and allowing it to rule your home. You must set rules and stick to them.

Another biggie is the internet! Does your husband have access to the internet at home, at his workplace or on his cell phone? His phone and computer must have a good internet filter—preferably one that also offers a reporting service. That way if he does manage to get around the filter somehow, you will get a report about what websites he's been into.

Lastly, you both must commit to regular attendance and meaningful participation in your local church.

These are all areas that the wife of a sexual addict should be involved with in her husband's life. As I already stated, holding your husband accountable for his sexual sin is better handled by a male friend. The best scenario would be for your husband to come to the Pure Life Ministries Residential Program—or at least to go through the Overcomers At-Home Program. You both could receive the counseling, encouragement and accountability that you need.

For the couple who, for whatever reason, feels that the wife should be the one to hold him accountable, the following guidelines are appropriate:

When he confesses struggles, don't insist on details. For instance, if one evening he tells you that he struggled with fantasy that day, you don't need to know what it was about specifically: e.g., what kind of girl she was. You don't need details!

When he does confess his struggles, you can't allow yourself to fall apart emotionally or yell at him or even lay a guilt trip on him. If he thinks he will be punished for his honesty, he will quit confessing his struggles to you. He doesn't want to hurt you, and he also doesn't want to be beaten up for being honest.

Not only must you control your feelings—which is very hard for any woman—but you must also show your appreciation for his honesty. Be supportive of his willingness to be vulnerable. Keep in mind how hard it is for a man to admit these things to a woman, especially to his wife. You must do your best not to bring up his past failures. Be a good listener, and do not take the role of merciless interrogator.

I think you can see by these guidelines why we strongly encourage couples to find someone outside the marriage as a source of accountability. Use whichever principles apply to your situation, Deanna. Do all that you do with compassion and grace. Be as supportive as you can. If he is sincere, one day you will reap the blessings of your efforts to support him. As Galatians 6:9 says, "And let us not lose heart in doing good, for in due time we shall reap if we do not grow weary."

DIVORCE

Dear Theresa,

It was unclear to me whether or not you were expecting me to respond to your letter in which you explained why you were filing for a divorce. Yet, I assume you wanted some feedback.

Divorce…it is an ugly word isn't it? It involves more than simply the legal dissolution of a marital contract. I believe it has eternal consequences because God says that He hates divorce. (Malachi 2:16) Furthermore, Jesus revealed God's heart concerning this issue when He said, "Because of your hardness of heart, Moses permitted you to divorce your wives; but from the beginning it has not been this way." (Matthew 19:9) In other words, divorce was never a part of God's original plan. It only occurs because of sin: either the sin of unfaithfulness or the sin of unnecessarily breaking a covenant that has been made before the Lord.

The divorce rate among Christians is at an all-time high nowadays. Many of these divorces were because of adultery, but many others occurred for no better reason than just wanting an easy escape from painful circumstances.

In your letter you justified divorce because your husband has "committed adultery in his heart." I'm sure that you know that when Jesus condoned divorce in Matthew 5:32 He was referring to those who were involved in ongoing, unrepentant fornication with another person. Although it is true that adultery begins in the heart, it seems like a stretch to say that your husband's mental struggles fit into this category.*

You said you've had to deal with this for two years now and "can't take it anymore." I could understand wanting a divorce if your husband had been involved in an affair all this time and had been unwilling to repent, but don't you feel like you're giving up too easily?

---

* There are some Christian leaders who believe that unrepentant involvement in pornography is a legitimate basis for divorce. We don't tend to think that is true, but they could be right. Whatever the case may be, divorce should only be pursued as a last resort.

Theresa, I encourage you really to seek the Lord about this before you proceed any further. Open up your heart to God's will. I think you will find that He will give you the grace to love and bear your husband. If you'll do this, you will find that the long-term benefits will far outweigh the temporary relief of divorce.

LOST RESPECT

Dear Jeri,

I hear the same thing from many women: "I have lost all respect for my husband."* I know how that feels because I experienced the same thing.

Women tend to look to the husband to be the strong one of the family, the one whom they can depend upon to exercise wise and stable leadership. Most women want to look up to their husbands. This becomes difficult when the husband becomes involved in shameful and degrading behavior. Such weakness and lack of self-control often provokes a sense of disdain in the wife's heart toward her husband.

I've even heard women say, "God must be so disgusted with him." Those words come from a self-righteous spirit. The Lord would be disappointed in such behavior, but even His disappointment is laced with love and compassion.†

Nevertheless, it is a challenge to follow a man you don't respect. Allow me to offer a couple of thoughts to consider. The first is that the Bible commands wives to respect their husbands. (Ephesians 5:33) The Greek word is *phobeo*, which comes from the word for fear. The KJV Bible translates it as reverence. How do you have reverence, or even respect, for a man involved in perversion? What helps us is that this is a biblical commandment—not an optional course if we feel like doing it. If it were based on how it felt, Paul might have said something like, "Wives, treat your husbands with respect when their actions show they are worthy of it." In the same way a citizen is required to treat with respect the position of a police officer, wives must respect the authority God has given the husband in the home.

Second, we must be in the right spirit ourselves. My husband has said, "The difference between a discerning heart

---

* For more on this subject, please see Chapter One, "The Hurting Wife."
† Of course, God's grace and compassion does not mean that an unrepentant sinner will escape judgment for his sin.

and a critical spirit is brokenness. When you have come to see your own sinful condition and need for God's grace, you will look at the sin in another's life with eyes of compassion." That is so true!

How do you deal with these overwhelming feelings in the meantime? Pray for him, treat him with kindness and support him as best as you can. Your feelings may or may not change, but your behavior can.

Entrust yourself to the Lord, Jeri. Do your best, stay in prayer and let the Lord strengthen you and fill you with His Holy Spirit.

THE MERCY LIFE

Dear Yolanda,

It is always such a joy to receive a letter like yours. In it, you said you wanted to know more about "the mercy life" that you have heard Steve refer to in some of his messages, and how you can apply it in your marriage. I can appreciate your struggle with this kind of teaching—that it doesn't seem right to show mercy to someone so full of sin.

I went through the same struggle myself. To me, it seemed wrong to be kind to someone who stayed in unrepentant sin. I felt I had to punish sin in some way—to let the sinner know I didn't approve of his actions. The whole concept of "love the sinner, hate the sin" was foreign to me and went against my nature. It wasn't until much later that I really came to see that it is "the kindness of God (that) leads you to repentance." (Romans 2:4)

None of us can comprehend God's mercy until we've really come to grips with our own sinful condition. The reason my husband and I embraced this "mercy life" is because we knew what sinners we were. Until you come to terms with your own need for mercy, it will have little or no real value to you. That is the problem so many of the women I deal with experience. They are looking at their husbands' sin rather than examining their own hearts. When I hear a wife say, "I don't do the things he does," I know she does not have a grasp of her own desperate condition. Getting saved doesn't somehow erase a person's fallen nature.

Once you see what a sinner you have been in life and how merciful God has been to you, the gratitude that wells up in your heart moves you to compassion for other sinners. Unfortunately, most Christians are quick to take God's mercy for themselves but are slow to offer it to others.

The "mercy life" is simply a description of what the Christian life is supposed to be. Extending mercy to another is primarily an act of meeting the needs of that person, looking for nothing in return. For someone thirsty, it is water. For the hungry, it is food. For the homeless, it might be clothing or shelter. For an unsaved relative, it means intercession or even sharing one's testimony. For a starving village in Africa, it could mean donating money, food or farm implements. For an orphan, it is financial aid or even adoption.

To live the "mercy life" means to allow God to use you to meet the needs of those He puts in your life. This could be formal ministry or simply the daily life of a true Christian.

In the context of being married to a man who is struggling with sexual sin, what do you think his greatest needs are? How could God use you to meet those needs?

I would say that holding him accountable in a spirit of love would be right at the top of the list. Encouraging him when he's down or giving him a strong exhortation when he sluffs off his responsibilities would both be considered merciful, if done in the right spirit. It is that compassionate attitude that makes the difference between extending God's love and frustrated nagging.

The greatest mercy you can do for Jesse, however, is to intercede for him regularly and continually. What could be more important than bombarding heaven on your husband's behalf? Not only will it have a great effect on him, as it enables God to work in his life, but, perhaps more importantly, it will help you to stay in the right spirit toward him. It's hard to be mad at someone you are pouring your heart out for every day.

I know you are praying for Jesse. I just want to encourage you to keep pressing in to God for his sake, and also for your own. The Lord is the only hope for your marriage and for your life.

LOST LOVE

Dear Diane,

I disagree with your statement that in God's eyes, your marriage is over because you don't love your husband anymore. That is not the heart of the Lord, Diane.

Believe me, I know what it's like to live with a man when the feelings are gone. It seems as though nothing can restore the love and respect again. There is little or no desire for reconciliation.

You say that you are friendly with him but have lost your romantic feelings for him. It seems that, in your mind, romantic feelings and love are synonymous. This is a worldly concept which many Christians have adopted. In his book, *At the Altar of Sexual Idolatry*, my husband gave the following illustration of this:

> Perhaps the reason Hollywood so readily promotes the adulterer is because it has such a superficial idea about what love is. In the movies, love is a tidal wave of emotion which overtakes a person almost against his or her own will. How many movies are there where the married woman helplessly "falls in love" with another man? She knows it is wrong, but she just cannot seem to help herself. Of course, the husband is always made to appear to be some monster so that everyone cheers when the anguished wife finally gives in to her feelings and commits adultery.[1]

From the world's perspective, a person's feelings dictate how they are to treat others. However, this is not the case for Christians who have a much higher calling. Jesus laid out the path for His followers when He said:

> But I say to you who hear, love your enemies, do good to those who hate you, bless those who curse you, pray

for those who mistreat you....Treat others the same way you want them to treat you. If you love those who love you, what credit is that to you? For even sinners love those who love them. (Luke 6:27-32)

Here we are given a clear-cut command from our Savior to love those who don't treat us the way we think we should be treated. But how can Jesus expect us to have warm feelings for those who curse and mistreat us? He doesn't. Although we can't control our feelings, we can control our words and actions.

In the great "love chapter" of First Corinthians 13, fifteen actions are laid out that sum up the word love for the believer. The wife may not have romantic feelings toward her husband, but there is nothing to stop her from being kind, humble, patient or even self-sacrificing with him. Again, to quote Steve:

The foundation of biblical love is based upon one's behavior, rather than one's feelings. When a man is being kind to his wife, for instance, he is loving her; thus, when he is being unkind to her, he is not loving her. Since love is a behavior which a person can choose to do, his emotions must always be secondary to his conduct. This is why Jesus could command His followers to love their enemies. He did not expect them to have warm and fuzzy feelings when others mistreated them.[2]

Well, I don't want to belabor the issue, but perhaps I can encourage you to do the following homework assignment: Make a commitment that for one month you will do everything within your ability to do things God's way. For thirty days you will set aside your feelings, your agenda and your plans. Consider this to be a project for the Lord. If nothing has changed for you and your husband after this period, then at that time you can reconsider your options. But during this timeframe, you are not even to think about divorce.

You must first come to the Lord with the right attitude, willing to allow Him to change your heart. If you just go through the motions and refuse to open your heart up to Him, this project is doomed from the start. Just ask the Lord to help you be willing to do His will.

Second, each morning throughout this month, during your devotional time, spend some time praying over First Corinthians 13:1-8 and Luke 6:27-46. Meditate and pray over each verse. Ask the Lord to make His words real to you. Ask Him to help you live out those words in your daily life.

During this one-month period, you must commit to living these words toward your husband. No one is expecting you to do this perfectly, but do the best you can, and do it with all of your heart.

Diane, you said in your letter that you were looking for the will of God for your life. I just want to remind you that it is always the will of God for a believer to treat others—even the unlovable—with love. The best way to stay in His will is to do His will wherever you are. Of course, if you are simply looking for an excuse to leave your marriage, then none of this will be of any interest to you. However, if you really meant what you said about wanting God's will, then this exercise will put you in the mindset of the Lord where you can better hear His voice. Then, if you feel that the Lord is leading you to divorce your husband, you will have the assurance that it truly is His will and not simply an angry reaction to his sin.

As I conclude this letter, allow me to speculate on the struggle you will have over doing what I have asked here for the next thirty days. Perhaps as you read my suggestion, an unwillingness rose up in your heart. If it is so, the basis of it is likely fear. Because you have been hurt and have already decided not to make yourself vulnerable to him any longer, the whole idea of giving yourself emotionally to your husband in this way probably struck dread in your heart.

What I want to help you see, Diane, is that you no longer feel love because you no longer want to give love. You have closed your heart to your husband and just want to get on with your life without him. What you may not realize though, is that whenever you close your heart to another person, you have closed it to God first.

I know you have been hurt and battered emotionally, but the healing you need will never come by running away from painful circumstances; it will come from the Lord as you remain in His Spirit. I'm not trying to beat up on you, sister. I'm trying to steer you away from a disastrous course.

In your mind you may have it all worked out. You will bring "closure" to this ugly chapter in your life and get on with your life. You feel that your marriage has been a mistake that you will now fix. What you will eventually discover is that you will face the same kinds of difficulties and conflicts in future relationships as well. If you don't learn how to love others unconditionally where you are, you will live a defeated life, never able to please the Lord and obey His command to "love your neighbor as yourself."

Humble yourself to the Lord, Diane, and allow Him to replace your thoughts with His thoughts and give you a new heart. Then, you will find joy and peace to see you through.

HIGH EXPECTATIONS

Dear Gloria,

Let me start by offering you words of warning: if you don't start being more compassionate and merciful to your husband, you are going to drive him right out the front door.

I guess that statement is an attention grabber! Please, don't take me wrong. My impression of you is that you are very intolerant of sin in both your own life as well as your husband's. It's certainly commendable to hold yourself to a high standard of godliness, but if you attempt to make the same demands on your husband you will find yourself buried in a pit of self-righteousness. If you do give over to that attitude, pretty soon you will be boasting along with the Pharisee, "God, I thank Thee that I am not like other people: swindlers, unjust, adulterers, or even like this tax-gatherer..." (Luke 18:11) You will find your husband beating his chest in humble repentance, while you go home unjustified.

I realize that your strong determination has helped you to overcome problems in your own life. However, not everyone progresses at the same rate and in the same way. You cannot lay down the ultimatum to your husband that "he better be in complete victory within three months, or it's over." That's unreasonable and rather unmerciful considering how much your husband will have to battle through.

This statement reveals a number of misconceptions about what God is like and what He expects from His children. First of all, He doesn't put those kinds of time limits on us. He knows how strong the hold is that sin can have on a person. The Bible says that God is longsuffering with our sin. That doesn't mean that He condones it. It means that He has so much love for the sinner that He is willing to endure with the person's acts of disobedience, as He is breaking the stronghold of those sins in his life.

God isn't intolerant of us, nor is He impatient with us when we're struggling. He loves us deeply and is willing to go to any lengths to discipline us for holiness. He is the surgeon of souls and goes inside our hearts to remove the cancer that would otherwise kill us.

People who demand holiness from others usually have very little comprehension of what true holiness really means. God doesn't live by some rigid set of rules that He never transgresses, therefore He is "perfect." The rules of the Bible stem from God's heart for meeting the needs of people and His desire that we, too, walk in His love toward others. Holy living stems from a love for God. Your outward works don't make you holy – it is love responding to Love.

Take the last six of the Ten Commandments, for instance. Each of these "rules" has to do with the way we treat other people. God doesn't ask us to keep these rules so we will be rigid Pharisees. He asks us to keep them out of a heart-felt obedience to Him and love and devotion for those other people.

I agree with you that your husband is being unloving toward the women he lusts over. While this is true, God is the only one who can help him to overcome that lust. Even if you were somehow able to police him into maintaining a lust-free life, most likely it would only mean that he became like the Pharisees. They kept the laws of God to look religious and receive the praise of men, not because they were so filled with love for others that they didn't want to hurt or use them. Lust is something your husband should struggle against, but ultimately it will be the love of God that uproots and supplants it.

If you are living a consecrated life, as you have claimed in your letter, that is wonderful! That consecration should be helping you be more like God, to see people as He sees them, to feel compassion over them as He does and to endure with their failures. It will also keep you in sight of your own great need. The change that occurs within you will hinder you from seeing yourself as better than others.

I think you should probably re-evaluate your stringent "guidelines and rules." I know that you were instructed by your counselors to set boundaries for your husband, but I have a feeling that you have gone a little overboard. How can you set a boundary on the mind of another human being? I think it is rather commendable that your husband has been so honest with you, considering how explosive you can be. I encourage you to be careful of your intolerance toward his struggles, or you will cause him to regret he ever opened up to you.

Why not humble yourself and go to him? Let him know that you were wrong in giving him an ultimatum and that you are going to support him through his struggles. This would mean a lot to him. You would do far more to help him overcome, than if you were to legislate rules into his life that he simply is not able to keep. May God bless you in your passion for holiness and your devotion to your husband and those around you. ᴖ

WATCHING PORNOGRAPHY

Dear Wanda,

You said in your letter that you are confused. I suspect this is exactly what your husband has been hoping for. Confusion wears down one's resistance to evil. The primary question of your letter was: "Is it wrong to view pornography with my husband in the privacy of our home?" In our "anything goes" society, most think that there is nothing at all wrong with it. But I assume you are looking for a biblical response from someone who has gone down that path.

Many years ago I was, like you, very confused and hurt. At the time, viewing pornography with Steve seemed to be the only way to keep him from being unfaithful to me. His argument that it was something we could enjoy together and, at the same time, would end any further sneaking around was very persuasive. I was so emotionally beaten down that I acquiesced to his wishes. I had no inkling then how untrue his arguments were. I was so short-sighted and shallow. I paid a heavy price spiritually and emotionally.

Initially things went well. Steve was genuinely grateful that he wouldn't have to sneak around anymore. In his sin-sick mind, I think he sincerely believed what he told me. At the beginning of this period, he treated me better than he had in years. But before long, the thrill of it began to dissipate—as sin always does—and he began sneaking out to massage parlors again. Then Steve suggested that we invite other people into our sex life. Again, in my obsessive desire to keep him, I reluctantly agreed. We both began to spiral downward. After just a few months of it, I became numb to this new fetish as well. My conscience was being seared. My sense of moral conviction was almost on empty. It was then that I finally realized I would have to leave him. I could not handle it anymore! I finally came to the place where I would rather be single than live like this. This was where I needed to be.

Had I only known what it would cost me, I never would have gotten involved in the first place. In my great determination to win my husband's love, no matter what, I was willing to sacrifice my self-respect, the morals I was raised with and most importantly, my walk with God. For years, I was riddled with guilt and shame over the things I had seen and done.

But that wasn't all. It took years for those images and unpleasant memories to go away. For some time, I had to deal with unnatural desires I had never experienced before. Pornographic movies create the illusion that every person alive is highly sexed and perverted. They warp a person's perspectives of other people. For a long time, I saw every woman as someone who wanted to seduce my husband and every man as a pervert.

Having said all this, allow me to ask you some penetrating questions. Do you think it is right to be so needy for a man that you would consider degrading yourself with pornography just to keep the relationship together? What kind of a person will you have to become to keep him happy? Are you really willing to involve yourself with and consent to your husband's secret perversions? Do you realize that becoming involved with pornography will only give your husband the license to openly lust over girls in your presence? Are you sure you are willing to subject yourself to that? Are you willing to involve yourself with something as evil and dark as pornography? Are you willing to walk away from God for the sake of appeasing your husband? Don't you realize that this will not cause him to love you more? Once you have hardened your heart against the Lord and filled your mind with perversion, what is going to stop you from taking the next step and the one after that? These are questions you better carefully consider before venturing one inch further down this path.

I believe your letter to me was a sincere plea for help. Pray for God's strength, put your foot down and tell your husband you are unwilling to become involved with his perversion.

The Importance of Gratitude

Dear Sylvia,

You wanted me to remind you again of why you should be grateful. I gather from your letter that you are struggling with an ungrateful and critical spirit. It is so hard to walk this narrow path at times, isn't it? I know I had my days when I just wanted to throw in the towel and say, "Forget it! I'm gonna be mad and bitter, and I'm gonna enjoy it—so just leave me alone!" It reminds me of a bad hair day. You get so frustrated, all you want to do is shave your head bald! Of course, you don't do it because you know tomorrow it will be better.

I have heard it said that a grateful heart is a full heart, and I have found it to be true. In fact, I would go so far as to say that the main reason for my present joy and my husband's victory over sexual sin is directly related to our level of gratitude. Had we never opened our eyes to see God's merciful dealings in our lives we would be full of misery, regret and defeat.

Please understand that you must choose to be grateful—it is something you do. Instead of allowing yourself to gripe and complain about all of the things in life that aren't right (which is very natural for the unconsecrated mind), you have to make the decision to declare all of the wonderful things that God has done for you. And guess what? You can't allow your feelings to dictate when you will be grateful. I understand; it's easier to see the negative and to believe the worst, but if you will determine to see God in the light of His goodness, your attitude will change despite your circumstances. And, of course, I could add that any sinner will be grateful when all life's circumstances line up with her desires. (cf. Luke 6:32) So it's all the more important for us to express gratitude when our circumstances are not so favorable, perhaps even painful.

The more you express gratitude in your heart, the more grateful you become. You begin to see how merciful God has been to you throughout your life—even when you were

His enemy. Gratitude is miraculous and changes everything. Being thankful keeps you in the same Spirit Jesus lived in while on earth.

What Paul taught is very true: You reap what you sow. If you cultivate a thankful heart, you will reap the joy and contentment that comes with it. Likewise, if you give over to a bitter and pessimistic spirit, you will reap an abundant harvest of misery. This misery, in turn, will affect every aspect of your life, especially your loved ones.

At the Pure Life Ministries residential program, a regular homework assignment for men dealing with self-pity or resentment is to write out a gratitude list of fifty things they are grateful for about the person or situation they have been grumbling about. This can be quite a challenge for those who are so accustomed to dwelling on negativity. But it is phenomenal how quickly a sincere person's outlook on life or a particular circumstance can change from such a simple assignment.

What keeps us defeated and in an ungrateful spirit is a lack of faith. Once you begin to see what the Lord is really like and how intimately involved He is in your life, you just want to sit down and thank Him for all that He has done for you.

There is so much to be thankful for. I could write an entire book on the subject. Just on a spiritual level, we can thank the Father for sending His Son. We can thank Jesus for leaving His throne, coming to this earth and dying on the cross for our sins. We can thank the Holy Spirit for carefully arranging the circumstances of our lives in order that we would see our need for God, convicting us of our sins at just the right time and leading us to the right church or person who helped us find the Lord.

We should also regularly thank God for all that He gives— for free! Such as? God gives us the keys to the kingdom (Matthew 16:19), the power to tread upon serpents (Luke 10:19), peace (John 14:27), eternal life (Romans 6:23), all things pertaining to life and godliness (2 Peter 1:3-4), spiritual gifts (1 Corinthians 12), knowledge of the mysteries of heaven (Matthew 13:11), power to become the sons of God (John 1:12), and the list goes on and on. Considering all these things, it is possible for a person to live in a spirit of gratitude all the time.

In your case, Sylvia, I encourage you to spend some time meditating upon all of the good God is doing for you through this difficult situation. Make out your own list. Just to give you a few examples: He is there as a refuge for you; He is trying to do good for you and your husband; He is showing both of you how much you need Him; He is deepening your faith, etc.

I can't say it enough: there is so much to be thankful for! One of the things we tell the men at the residential program is that for everything we can see that the Lord has done for us, there are a hundred other things that we don't even know about. It is so important to cultivate a grateful heart, because it helps a person put things in proper perspective.

God has nothing but good for you, Sylvia. Wouldn't it be better to express your gratitude to Him regularly for His kindness than to be a habitual complainer? You can choose to be grateful! God is for you and will grant you the grace to endure and bring you through this difficult situation.

DEALING WITH UNFORGIVENESS

Dear Rita,

I appreciate your seeking advice as to how to forgive someone who's hurt you so deeply. You said that people have accused you of being unforgiving because you still struggle with certain feelings directly related to your husband's infidelity. Let me tell you Rita, as well-intentioned as some people may be, many of them do not understand the depth of your pain. They have no idea how devastating your husband's struggle with sexual sin has been to you. It is not necessarily unforgiveness you are struggling with. You are just human and are still working through some very serious issues.

You seem to be a very sincere Christian woman who desires to please the Lord. In your letter, you did not come across vindictive at all. Your statement, "I want to be healed, and I want my husband healed so that we can be pleasing to the Lord together," doesn't sound like a woman full of bitterness.

So on that basis, I will address your question. Jesus dealt less with outward behavior and more with people's hearts. With precision, He went right to the root issue buried deep within. Like a two-edged sword His words pierced through, dividing the soul and spirit, judging the thoughts and intents of the heart. In Matthew 5, when He talked about heart adultery, He was showing lust-filled men the depravity of their hearts. It was the same thing with anger. He said that if you are angry at someone, you are in the exact same spirit as a murderer. The words of Jesus expose our hearts and reveal what hypocrites we can be. We judge according to outward appearances, but God looks upon the heart.

Forgiveness is the same. I realize you are struggling with feelings of betrayal and bitterness. Who wouldn't, considering what you've had to endure? You are right now in the process of fighting through some very painful issues that have been devastating. Please understand that feelings come and go, but the Lord is more concerned with what is occurring in your heart. From what you expressed in your letter, it seems to me that you simply want the best for your husband. Yes, you have those times of anger, but for the most part you sincerely desire to see him get free. You love him and want him to make it. You don't bring up the past and throw it in his face.

Forgiveness is a process that takes time. I don't mean to imply that we are excused for ever being unforgiving. What I mean is that it takes time for the wife to feel like she can trust her husband again. Because he is the one who broke that trust, the burden is on his shoulders to re-establish a relationship built upon trust and truthfulness.

The forgiving wife wants her husband to make it, does everything she can to encourage him and therefore expects him to take the situation seriously. A wife who is unforgiving, on the other hand, continually reminds him of his past offenses and anticipates his constant failure. This, of course, only serves to further demoralize him and retard his efforts to get free. The idol in the heart of an unforgiving wife is s-e-l-f. She is far more concerned about protecting herself from ever being hurt again, than she is about restoring her marriage or supporting her husband in his struggle to overcome sexual sin.

Don't be too hard on yourself, Rita. It seems that the two of you are well on your way to putting this whole, ugly affair behind you. God will help you get through it. The feelings of anger will subside, and your heart will open up to your husband once again. You'll have to continue to show patience to your husband—and to yourself!

ENDNOTES

CHAPTER 1

1 Steve Gallagher, *At the Altar of Sexual Idolatry* (Dry Ridge, KY: Pure Life Ministries, 2007), pps 40-41.

CHAPTER 4

1 George Barna, *Real Teens: A Contemporary Snapshot of Youth Culture* (Ventura, CA: Regal, 2001), p 26.

2 American Academy of Pediatrics Committee on Public Education, "Sexuality, Contraception, and the Media," *Pediatrics*, vol. 107, issue 1 (January, 2001), accessed at http://pediatrics.aappublications. org/content/107/1/191 on July 13, 2018.

CHAPTER 5

1 Rex Andrews, *What the Bible Teaches About Mercy* (Zion, IL: The Zion Faith Homes, 1985), p. 157-158.

CHAPTER 7

1 Steve Gallagher, *A Biblical Guide to Counseling the Sexual Addict* (Dry Ridge, KY: Pure Life Ministries, 2005), pps 45-46.

CHAPTER 8

1 Lloyd Oglivie, *Facing the Future without Fear* (Ann Arbor, MI: Servant Publications, 1999), as cited at http://www. soulshepherding.org/fear-not-365-days-a-year/ accessed on July 21, 2018.

CHAPTER 9

1 Marlo Thomas, as quoted by The Quote Garden, accessed at http:// quotegarden.com/feminism.html on July 14, 2018.

2 Erica Jong, as quoted by The Quote Garden, accessed at http:// quotegarden.com/feminism.html on July 14, 2018.

3 Isadora Duncan, as quoted by The Quote Garden, accessed at

http://quotegarden.com/feminism.html on July 14, 2018.

4 Bertrand Russell, *Marriage and Morals*, as quoted by The Quote Garden, accessed at http://quotegarden.com/feminism.html on July 14, 2018.

5 Cynthia Heimel, *Sex Tips for Girls*, as quoted by The Quote Garden, accessed at http://quotegarden.com/feminism.html on July 14, 2018.

6 John MacArthur, sermon transcript of "An Excellent Wife" (May 8, 1988), accessed at https://www.gty.org/library/sermons-library/80-50/an-excellent-wife on July 14, 2018.

7 A.W. Pink, "The Cross and Self" (June 1930), accessed at http://articles.ochristian.com/article717.shtml on July 14, 2018.

LOST LOVE

1 Steve Gallagher, *At the Altar of Sexual Idolatry* (Dry Ridge, KY: Pure Life Ministries, 2007), pps 255-256.

2 Steve Gallagher, *At the Altar of Sexual Idolatry* (Dry Ridge, KY: Pure Life Ministries, 2007), p. 257.

PURE LIFE MINISTRIES

Pure Life Ministries helps Christian men achieve lasting freedom from sexual sin. The Apostle Paul said, "Walk in the Spirit and you will not fulfill the lust of the flesh." Since 1986, Pure Life Ministries (PLM) has been discipling men into the holiness and purity of heart that comes from a Spirit-controlled life. At the root, illicit sexual behavior is sin and must be treated with spiritual remedies. Our counseling programs and teaching resources are rooted in the biblical principles that, when applied to the believer's daily life, will lead him out of bondage and into freedom in Christ.

BIBLICAL TEACHING RESOURCES

Pure Life Ministries offers a full line of books, audio CDs and DVDs specifically designed to give men the tools they need to live in sexual purity.

RESIDENTIAL CARE

The most intense and involved counseling PLM offers comes through the **Residential Program** (9 months), in Dry Ridge, Kentucky. The godly and sober atmosphere on our 45-acre campus provokes the hunger for God and deep repentance that destroys the hold of sin in men's lives.

HELP AT HOME

The **Overcomers At-Home Program** (OCAH) is available for those who cannot come to Kentucky for the Residential Program. This twelve-week counseling program features weekly counseling sessions and many of the same teachings offered in the Residential Program.

CARE FOR WIVES

Pure Life Ministries also offers help to wives of men in sexual sin through our 12-week **At-Home Program for Wives**. Our wives' counselors have suffered through the trials and storms of such a discovery and can offer a devastated wife a sympathetic ear and the biblical solutions that worked in their lives.

PURE LIFE MINISTRIES
14 School St. • Dry Ridge • KY • 41035
Office: 859.824.4444 • Orders: 888.293.8714
inform@purelifeministries.org
www.purelifeministries.org

THE WALK SERIES

BIBLE STUDIES FOR PERSONAL GROWTH AND GROUP DISCIPLESHIP

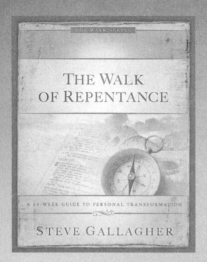

THE WALK OF REPENTANCE

A 24-week Bible study for the Christian who wants to be more deeply consecrated to God. Experience the times of spiritual refreshing that follow repentance.

Spanish Version also available!

A LAMP UNTO MY FEET

A 12-week journey through the beautiful Psalm 119 and the life of David. Every reader will be brought into a deeper love, respect and appreciation for God's Word.

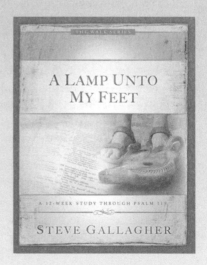

HE LEADS ME BESIDE STILL WATERS

A practical study of the choicest Psalms. This 12-week study takes you right into the intimate interactions between pious men and a loving, caring God and evokes a determined desire to find His Presence for yourself.

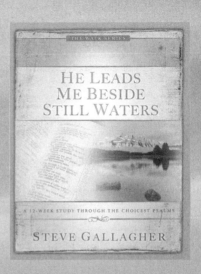

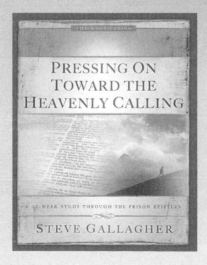

PRESSING ON TOWARD THE HEAVENLY CALLING

The Prison Epistles are a divine archive of profound revelations about the kingdom of God. This 12-week study will challenge you to reach for the abundant life in God that Paul testifies is available to every one of us.

THESE BOOKS WILL FOREVER CHANGE YOUR PERSPECTIVE OF THE END TIMES CHURCH

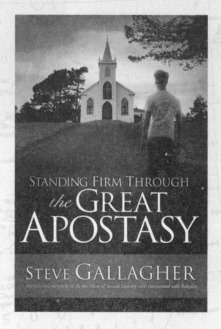

From the outset, the implications of this book are terrifying. In this thorough, and sometimes disquieting, investigation of biblical predictions, the Great Apostasy emerges, not as a foreboding future event, but as the very essence of today's postmodern church.

Like tares in the wheat field, false adherents are presently growing up alongside true believers. But how will we know them? What are the distinguishing qualities of these apostate confessors?

This is where Steve Gallagher is at his best. By mining the treasure-laden writings of past centuries and carefully examining the sacred Scriptures, he exposes the prevailing self-centeredness, widespread sensuality, and rebellion to authority that epitomizes this false part of the Body.

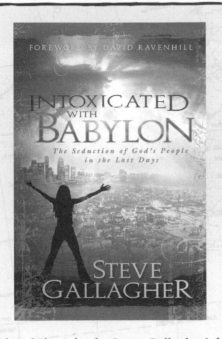

OTHER BOOKS AVAILABLE

BY PURE LIFE MINISTRIES

At the Altar of Sexual Idolatry
At the Altar of Sexual Idolatry DVD Curriculum
At the Altar of Sexual Idolatry Workbook
A Biblical Guide to Counseling the Sexual Addict
Create in Me a Pure Heart
Entering His Courts
From Ashes to Beauty
He Leads Me Beside Still Waters
How America Lost Her Innocence
i: the root of sin exposed
Intoxicated with Babylon
A Lamp Unto My Feet
Living in Victory
Out of the Depths of Sexual Sin
Pressing on Toward the Heavenly Calling
Selah! The Book of Psalms in the Richest Translations
Standing Firm through the Great Apostasy
The Time of Your Life in Light of Eternity
The Walk of Repentance
Wisdom: Proverbs & Ecclesiastes in the Richest Translations
The Word of Their Testimony